58 Orecchiette with Sweet Red Pepper Sauce

97 Carnitas Tacos

140 Tarragon Shrimp Skewers

166 Chicken with Peach and Melon Salsa

218 Tropical Trifle

This

Sandra Lee
semi-homemade®
20-minute meals 2

book belongs to:

....

Special thanks to Culinary Director Jeff Parker

Meredith® Books Des Moines, Iowa

Copyright © 2007 Sandra Lee Semi-Homemade® All rights reserved. Printed in the USA.
Library of Congress Control Number 2007929216 ISBN: 978-0-696-23816-1

sem·i·home·made

adj. **1:** a stress-free solution-based formula that provides savvy shortcuts and affordable, timesaving tips for overextended do-it-yourself homemakers **2:** a quick and easy equation wherein 70% ready-made convenience products are added to 30% fresh ingredients with creative personal style, allowing homemakers to take 100% of the credit for something that looks, feels, or tastes homemade **3:** a foolproof resource for having it all—and having the time to enjoy it **4:** a method created by Sandra Lee for home, garden, crafts, beauty, food, fashion, and entertaining wherein everything looks, tastes, and feels as if it was made from scratch.

Solution-based **E**nterprise that **M**otivates, **I**nspires, and **H**elps **O**rganize and **M**anage time, while **E**nriching **M**odern life by **A**dding **D**ependable shortcuts **E**very day.

dedication

To the Home Hero—
For making every family meal matter.
I hope this book provides
you with the extra time to
sit and enjoy yourself.
You are amazing every day!

To my Aunt Peggy—
For all of your love and support,
for Aspen, and for the special sundress
so many summers ago.
-xoxoxo SL

Table of Contents

Letter from Sandra 7

Sandra's Savvy Secrets 8

Shortcut Solutions for
    Breakfast and Lunch 10

Sandra's Select Tools 12

Quick-to-Mix Cocktails 14

Chapter 1

Starters
and Snacks
16

Chapter 2

Pasta
32

Chapter 5

Chicken and
Turkey
158

Chapter 3

Beef, Pork,
and Lamb
66

Chapter 6

Treats and
Desserts
206

Chapter 4

Fish and
Shellfish
112

Letter from Sandra

Time. It's the commodity we value most, but control least. Whether we're young or old, work in an office or work at home, we all have only 24 hours in a day. What we can control is how we spend the hours we have. Semi-Homemade® makes mealtime fun for everybody, helping all of us do more with less time and less money. There's always time to cook—when you can do it in just 20 minutes!

This book grew out of many hours—two decades, really—of seeking creative ways to cook quicker without sacrificing taste. Since I was a little girl, I've had a knack for shortcuts. Growing up, I was the oldest of five children. I was cooking and cleaning from the time I could turn on the stove. I realized that if I wanted to have any time left for myself, I'd better figure out how to get it all done quicker.

Looking back, I think my Semi-Homemade® philosophy was born right then. I'd pore over every recipe in the cookbooks I loved, with an eye toward streamlining. What tricks could I use to speed up the prep work? How could I doctor packaged products to make them taste homemade? It all added up to my unique 70/30 philosophy: Mix 70% quality readymade foods with 30% fresh ingredients, add a dash of creativity and cook up a meal that's 100% amazing! It's a formula that works for everyone, from busy parents to busy professionals—and especially those who manage to be both in one!

Like my first *Semi-Homemade® 20-Minute Meals* cookbook, this book makes the most of every minute, offering six chapters of inventive recipes, conveniently paired into fabulous full-menu meals you can put together quickly and easily, with time to spare. In just one book you'll find everything you need to complete a meal, from snacks and starters to entrees, desserts, and more—even cocktails. There's party food, family food, everyday food, and special food—each easy to make with easy-to-find ingredients.

I love to cook… but I don't love spending hours in the kitchen. Time if the currency of life and much more valuable than money. Spend it wisely with Semi-Homemade®.

Cheers to a happy, healthy life!

Sandra Lee

Sandra's Savvy Secrets

Figuring out the main-dish was no problem—but what can you serve on the side? Save yourself loads of time by tweaking and sprucing up the best of the best in convenience products. The fabulous results will complete the meal—all in under 20 minutes!

Simple Side Dishes

Ready Rice: Just vent the bag, pop it in the microwave, and in a minute or two piping hot rice is ready to go. Go south of the border by adding heated black beans, canned tomatoes, corn, cilantro, and a dash of cumin.

Refrigerated Mashed Potatoes: Here's a favorite of everyone—comfort food at its best in no time flat. Add some simple stir-ins, such as crisp-cooked prosciutto and shredded cheese, or sour cream and fresh chopped chives or other herbs.

Refrigerated Cubed Potatoes: What's a picnic without potato salad? Make it quick by combining these potatoes with mayo, mustard, celery, and onion.

Refrigerated Pasta: Cook these products according to the package directions, then add purchased Alfredo sauce, scallions, and bacon pieces.

Mediterranean salad

Speedy potato salad

Mexican-style rice

Add some veggies

Bagged Salad Mixes: It's all in the toppings. Try crowning your lettuce with feta cheese, roasted red peppers, olives, artichoke hearts, and a vinaigrette.

Frozen and Microwaveable Vegetables: All they need is a little butter, but another time try sprucing up your favorites with fresh herbs or spices. And if you add a little cheese, everyone will beg for more.

9

Shortcut Solutions for Breakfast and Lunch

This book is packed with fast dinner and dessert ideas—but what about morning and afternoon? Here's some thoughts to start you off. Once you get these down, start trying your own ideas!

Spruced-up tuna salad

Tortellini-salami salad

Morning and Noon

Now you can have it all—in minutes! Delicious breakfasts and lunches can be made in 20 minutes or less too, so no more excuses.

Breakfast: Try toasted frozen waffles drizzled with yogurt and fresh berries or coated with apple butter and pecans. For something savory, use a tortilla to wrap up scrambled eggs, precooked bacon, and cheese, or top a toasted English muffin with a fried egg, ham, and cheese. Then take it to go!

Lunch: Forget PB&J. Go for glam by combining cooked cheese tortellini, salami, cheese, olives, tomatoes, and vinaigrette. Or re-do plain ol' tuna sandwiches by combining tuna with mayo, scallions, fresh tarragon, and lemon juice—all on ciabatta bread. If you're taking it for later, remember to use a frozen cooler pack and an insulated bag.

Waffles with yogurt and fruit

Breakfast wrap with bacon

11

Sandra's Select Tools

You just can't have too many snazzy kitchen tools—especially if they're made of silicone! You can now find this heat-resistant, easy-to-clean material coating every utensil—including tongs, basting brushes, spatulas, whisks, measuring cups, and more!

Gotta Have It!

Everyone has a beloved kitchen tool they just can't cook without—here are five of my absolute favorites.

Small cookie sheets: These tiny pans are perfect for baking small batches of cookies. And you'll never have a problem finding room to store them.

Pasta drainer: For one-handled pots, this strainer is ideal. No need to hassle with a clunky colander and cleanup is faster!

Santoku knives: I love chopping with these easy-to-hold knives. Slices of veggies slide right off because of the scalloped edges on the blades.

Cutting board with tray: A cook's dream! With a built-in tray, transporting food from cutting board to pot is simple.

Y-shape peeler: Make beautiful vegetable curls with this easy-to-use peeler. You can also use it to make chocolate curls.

Small cookie sheets

Pasta Strainer

Cutting board and Santoku knives

Y-shape peeler

Quick-to-Mix Cocktails

Even cocktails can be quicker than ever before. You can purchase drink products that contain everything (including the alcohol) or mixes that require the quick addition of liquor. Serve these as easy pre-party treats or after-dinner sippers.

Tom Collins and Piña Colada Mixes

Liquors for mixing

Party Time!

It's always a good time to gather with friends for a cocktail.

A Mix for Every Occasion

Premade mixes make cocktail time easy. For extra flair, garnish your cocktails to the hilt.

Margaritas: The tequila is already mixed into the Golden Margarita mix—just blend with ice and garnish with limes.

Bloody Mary: Serve over ice, and garnish with olives, pickles, celery, and more.

Daiquiri and Mai Tai: Fresh fruit tops these frosty beverages.

Tom Collins: Serve this drink on the rocks with a cherry and some citrus twists.

Piña Colada: Top with a spear of cherries and pineapple.

Whiskey Sour: Garnish with mint, citrus twists, and a cherry.

Manhattan: This is sophistication in a glass—perfect for the high-falutin' friends in your life.

Whiskey Sour and Manhattan mixes

Daiquiri and Mai Tai mixes

15

Starters and Snacks

There's something about beginnings. Maybe it's the clean plate that lures me or maybe it's the promise that lovely as this dish is, it's just a sample of more to come. Whatever the appeal, you have to start somewhere … and this chapter is a wonderful place. If you're looking for small bites with big flavor, try Crostini with Shrimp and *Boursin* Cheese. When company's coming, Fried Cheese Ravioli with Tomato Pepper Relish lets you impress with ease. And Chicken Caesar Focaccia Sandwiches combine salad and sandwich in one—just the thing for today's on-the-go lifestyle. Each dish is wonderfully flexible, so fix a single-serving snack, combine a couple into a casual meal, or line up a beautiful buffet for your next party.

The Recipes

Greek Layered Dip with Pita Chips	18
Fried Cheese Ravioli with Tomato Pepper Relish and Artichoke Caper Dip	21
Crab Cake Fritters	22
Crostini with Shrimp and *Boursin* Cheese	25
Prosciutto-Tied Asparagus	25
Chili Cheese Slices	26
Artichoke Focaccini	26
Chicken Caesar Focaccia Sandwiches with Rosemary Skewers	29
Creamy Chicken Mini Pitas	29
Tea Sandwiches Two Ways	
Roast Beef and Blue Cheese	
French Brie and Ham Baguette	30

Greek Layered Dip with Pita Chips

Start to Finish 20 minutes
Makes 10 servings

Hot, spicy dips are quick to make—and quick to vanish. Ground lamb, hummus, feta cheese, and vegetables, teamed with a basket of baked pita chips, offer all the food groups in one. Make it a healthy mini meal or a warm-up for a light supper.

1	package (14-ounce) pita bread, *Sara Lee*®
	olive oil cooking spray
4	teaspoons Greek seasoning, divided, *Spice Islands*®
1	pound ground lamb
1	teaspoon garlic salt, *Lawry's*®
1	container (16-ounce) premade hummus, *Athenos*®
1½	cups tzatziki (gyro sauce), *Sahara*®
1	cup shredded iceberg lettuce, *Ready Pac*®
2	medium Roma tomatoes, diced
½	cup diced red onion, *Ready Pac*®
½	cup Kalamata olives, chopped
1	container (4-ounce) crumbled feta cheese, *Athenos*®

1. Preheat oven to 375 degrees F. Line one or two baking sheets with foil. Cut pita bread into eighths. Split each piece in two and place on prepared baking sheet, inside of bread face up. Spray with olive oil cooking spray and sprinkle with 2 teaspoons of the Greek seasoning. Bake for 7 to 10 minutes, or until golden.

2. Meanwhile, in a large skillet, brown ground lamb with garlic salt and the remaining 2 teaspoons Greek seasoning. Drain and set aside. In a shallow 1½ quart baking dish, spread hummus on the bottom. Top with a layer of ground lamb. Top with tzatziki. Layer with remaining ingredients in order listed. Serve dip at room temperature with baked pita chips.

Fried Cheese Ravioli with Tomato Pepper Relish and Artichoke Caper Dip

Start to Finish 20 minutes
Makes 4 servings

Instead of fried mozzarella, please all palates with this bistro-meets-bar snack. Four-cheese ravioli is pan-fried to a golden crisp and served with a choice of chunky, peppery tomato relish or cool, creamy artichoke caper dip.

	Vegetable oil, for frying
1	**package (9-ounce) four cheese ravioli,** *Buitoni*®

FOR TOMATO PEPPER RELISH

1	**cup roasted red peppers, drained, finely chopped,** *Mezzetta*®
¼	**cup diced tomatoes, drained, finely chopped,** *S&W*®
1	**tablespoon light brown sugar,** *C&H*®
1	**teaspoon balsamic vinegar**

FOR ARTICHOKE CAPER DIP

1	**jar (6.5-ounce) marinated artichoke hearts, drained, finely chopped,** *Mezzetta*®
2	**teaspoons capers**
2	**teaspoons mayonnaise,** *Best Foods*®
2	**tablespoons sour cream**
1	**tablespoon grated Parmesan cheese,** *DiGiorno*®
1	**teaspoon lemon juice,** *ReaLemon*®

1. In a straight-sided skillet, heat 2 inches of oil over medium-high heat. (The oil is ready when a drop of water splatters in the skillet.) When oil is ready, carefully fry ravioli until golden brown, about 1 minute per side. Drain on a paper towel-lined plate.

2. For tomato pepper relish, combine red peppers and tomatoes in a small bowl. Stir in brown sugar and balsamic vinegar and set aside.

3. For artichoke caper dip, combine artichoke hearts, capers, mayonnaise, sour cream, Parmesan cheese, and lemon juice in a small bowl. Serve ravioli hot with Tomato Pepper Relish and Artichoke Caper Dip.

Crab Cake Fritters

Start to Finish 20 minutes
Makes 8 servings

Old Bay® seasoning gives these bite-size crab cakes their zing. Dunked in a spiced tartar sauce they make a fun finger food, or stuff them in a French roll with sauce-drizzled veggies to make a New Orleans-style po'boy.

FOR CRAB CAKES
- ¾ cup panko bread crumbs
- Vegetable oil, for frying
- 2 cans (6 ounces each) lump crabmeat, drained, *Crown Prince*®
- 2 tablespoons mayonnaise, *Best Foods*®
- 1 egg
- 2 teaspoons lemon juice, *ReaLemon*®
- ½ teaspoon seafood seasoning, *Old Bay*®
- ¼ teaspoon celery salt

FOR SAUCE
- ⅔ cup tartar sauce, *Ken's*®
- 2 tablespoons Dijon mustard, *Grey Poupon*®
- ½ teaspoon seafood seasoning, *Old Bay*®

1. For crab cakes, pour ½ cup of the panko bread crumbs into a shallow dish and set aside. In a large skillet, heat 1 inch oil over medium-high heat. (The oil is ready when a drop of water splatters in the skillet.)

2. In a medium bowl, mix together all crab cake ingredients with remaining ¼ cup panko bread crumbs. Form into 1½-inch balls. Roll balls in reserved panko bread crumbs until well coated.

3. When oil is ready, carefully slide crab cake fritters into skillet. Fry until golden brown, turning often, about 4 to 5 minutes. Drain on a paper towel-lined plate.

4. For sauce, combine all sauce ingredients in a small bowl. Serve on the side of crab cake fritters.

Tip: Panko is coarsely ground, Japanese-style bread crumbs. Look for them in the Asian section of your supermarket.

Crostini with Shrimp and *Boursin* Cheese

Start to Finish 20 minutes
Makes 8 servings

24	baguette slices, ¼-inch thick
½	cup butter
1½	teaspoons crushed garlic, *Christopher Ranch*®
1	pound frozen cooked and peeled large shrimp (26/30 count), thawed
2	tablespoons chopped fresh parsley
1	package (5.2-ounce) soft cheese with garlic and herbs, *Boursin*®
12	cherry tomatoes, cut in half
	Chopped fresh chives (optional)

1. Preheat oven to 400 degrees F. Place baguette slices on a baking sheet and toast in preheated oven until just golden around the edges, about 7 to 10 minutes.

2. Meanwhile, melt butter in a large skillet over medium heat. Add garlic and sauté for 1 minute. Add shrimp and heat through, about 5 minutes. Add parsley and toss to combine. Remove from heat and set aside.

3. Spread toasted baguette slices with Boursin cheese and top with a shrimp and a cherry tomato half. Garnish with chopped chives (optional).

Prosciutto-Tied Asparagus

Start to Finish 20 minutes
Makes 18 bundles

In a nod to nouvelle cuisine, graceful asparagus takes a bow—with colorful prosciutto. The artful presentation makes a pretty plate for company or is a fun way to coax kids—and everybody else—into trying something different.

1	pound thin asparagus, ends trimmed
1	package (3-ounce) prosciutto, *Columbus*®
2	tablespoons extra virgin olive oil
1	teaspoon lemon juice, *ReaLemon*®
	Salt and pepper

1. Preheat oven to 400 degrees F. Line a baking sheet with foil. Cut prosciutto slices lengthwise into two thin strips. Gather two to three asparagus spears and carefully tie prosciutto into a knot around asparagus bundle. Continue until all ingredients are used and place asparagus bundles on prepared baking sheet.

2. In a small bowl, whisk together olive oil and lemon juice. Drizzle over asparagus. Season to taste with salt and pepper. Roast in preheated oven for 8 to 10 minutes.

Chili Cheese Slices

Start to Finish 20 minutes
Makes 8 servings

Zesty cheddar cheese chili served open-face on a buttery crescent roll is hearty enough to pinch hit as lunch or an afterschool snack. Kids love it and so will you—just open and layer five ingredients and you're done!

1 can (8-ounce) crescent rolls, *Pillsbury*®
  Nonstick cooking spray
¾ cup no-bean chili, *Hormel*®
¾ cup shredded cheddar cheese, *Kraft*®
4 teaspoons diced red onion, *Ready Pac*®
¼ cup sliced black olives, drained, *Early California*®

1. Preheat oven to 425 degrees F. Line a baking sheet with foil. Unroll crescent rolls and separate into 6 triangles. Place on prepared baking sheet and spray tops with cooking spray.

2. Top each slice with chili, cheddar cheese, onion, and olives. Bake for 12 to 15 minutes, or until edges are golden and cheese is melted.

Artichoke Focaccini

Start to Finish 20 minutes
Makes 4 servings

  Nonstick cooking spray
1 tablespoon extra virgin olive oil
1 teaspoon minced garlic, *Christopher Ranch*®
1 teaspoon Italian seasoning, *McCormick*®
1 can (16.3-ounce) refrigerated biscuit dough, *Pillsbury Grands*®
2 jars (6 ounces each) marinated artichoke hearts, drained, *Mezzetta*®
½ cup crumbled blue cheese, *Treasure Cave*®

1. Preheat oven to 350 degrees F. Lightly coat baking sheet with cooking spray and set aside. In a small bowl, combine olive oil, garlic, and Italian seasoning.

2. Unroll and separate biscuit dough. Shape each biscuit into ¼-inch thick rounds. Place on prepared baking sheet and make "dimples" in each round with fingertips.

3. Use a pastry brush to brush tops with olive oil mixture. Place 2 artichoke quarters on each round and top with 2 tablespoons crumbled blue cheese. Bake for 13 to 15 minutes, or until golden brown. Serve warm.

Chicken Caesar Focaccia Sandwiches with Rosemary Skewers

Start to Finish 10 minutes
Makes 8 sandwiches

1   bag caesar salad kit, *Fresh Express®*
½   package (6-ounce) grilled chicken strips, chopped, *Oscar Mayer®*
1   loaf focaccia bread
8   cherry tomatoes
8   (4-inch) rosemary sprigs

1. In a large bowl, combine all contents of salad kit and chicken strips. Toss to combine. Cut focaccia loaf in half horizontally. Fill focaccia bread with chicken Caesar salad. Cut focaccia sandwich into 8 portions.

2. Take each rosemary stalk and strip bottom half of the rosemary from the stalk, leaving leaves at top. Insert rosemary skewers through tomatoes. Insert each rosemary-tomato skewer into the top of each sandwich.

Creamy Chicken Mini Pitas

Start to Finish 20 minutes
Makes 30 pitas

1   store-bought roasted chicken
½   cup finely chopped celery
2   scallions, finely chopped
½   cup walnuts, finely chopped
1   tablespoon finely chopped fresh tarragon
1⅓   cups mayonnaise, *Best Foods®*
    Salt and pepper
15   mini pita breads, *Thomas' Sahara®*

1. Remove skin from chicken and pull meat from bones. Discard skin and bones, along with any excess fat. Chop meat into bite-size pieces.

2. In a medium bowl, combine chicken, celery, scallions, walnuts, tarragon, and mayonnaise. Mix thoroughly. Season to taste with salt and pepper.

3. Slice mini pitas in half. Open pockets and stuff with a heaping tablespoon of chicken mixture.

Roast Beef and Blue Cheese Tea Sandwiches

Start to Finish 10 minutes
Makes 12 half-sandwiches

⅓   cup blue cheese, crumbled, *Treasure Cave*®
½   cup mayonnaise, *Best Foods*®
1   tablespoon lemon juice, *ReaLemon*®
½   pound deli-sliced roast beef
1   bunch watercress
6   slices whole wheat bread
6   slices white bread

1. In a small bowl, stir together crumbled blue cheese, mayonnaise, and lemon juice.

2. Spread blue cheese mayonnaise on wheat bread slices. Add watercress and roast beef. Place white bread slice on top. Cut off crusts and slice into quarters diagonally.

French Brie and Ham Baguette Tea Sandwiches

Start to Finish 10 minutes
Makes 18 small sandwiches

1   (18-to 20-inch) baguette
⅓   cup peach or raspberry preserves, *Smucker's*®
1   package (6-ounce) deli ham slices, *Hillshire Farm*®
1   wedge (5-ounce) Brie, room temperature, *Alouette*®

1. Slice baguette horizontally with a serrated bread knife. Spread preserves on both halves of bread. On bottom half of baguette, lay down overlapping slices of ham and top with slices of Brie.

2. Place top of baguette on sandwich. Cut into 1-inch pieces and secure with decorative sandwich picks. Optional: heat in a 400 degree F oven for 10 to 12 minutes before serving.

Pasta

Life is full of choices, though few as gratifying as a meal in New York's Little Italy. For starters, I stroll up and down Mulberry Street, where sidewalk barkers hover outside homey trattorias, promising the best linguine… fettuccini… ravioli this side of Sicily. This chapter lets you sample them all, adapting Old World recipes for New World lifestyles right in your own cucina. When the weather's chilly—or appetites hearty—turn to the sauces of the south, like a tomato-rich Penne Puttanesca. A light wine sauce is the base for delicate Chicken Pasta Milanese, a full-course meal alongside Mixed Greens with Mandarin Oranges and Walnuts. When you're craving a cream sauce, Linguine with Vegetable Alfredo is too satisfying to miss the meat. Whatever you choose, raise your Chianti high and say salute! to the simple pleasure of pasta.

The Meals

Chicken Pasta Milanese	34
Mixed Greens with Mandarin Oranges and Walnuts	37
Mozzarella Garlic Bread	37
Fettucini with Lobster Sauce	38
Haricots Verts with Shaved Parmesan	38
Linguine with Vegetable Alfredo	41
Warm Spinach Salad with Eggs and Bacon	42
Linguine with Zucchini Caponata	45
Fresh Broccoli Salad	46
Prosciutto-Wrapped Breadsticks	46
Angel Hair with Salmon in Lemon Cream Sauce	49
Garlicky Sautéed Green Beans and Peas	49

Penne Niçoise	50
Arugula Salad with Pears and Gorgonzola	50
Penne Puttanesca	53
Zucchini al Formaggio	53
Bow Ties with Artichoke Pesto	54
Balsamic Roasted Tomatoes	57
Orecchiete with Sweet Red Pepper Sauce	58
Salad Bar Stir-Fry	61
Ravioli Balsamico	62
Roasted Asparagus with Portobello Mushrooms	62
Ravioli with Marsala-Caper Sauce	65
Sautéed Zucchini with Garlic and Herbs	65

Chicken Pasta Milanese

Start to Finish 20 minutes
Makes 4 servings

Serving Ideas:
Mixed Greens with
Mandarin Oranges
and Walnuts
(page 37)

Mozzarella Garlic
Bread (page 37)

12	ounces refrigerated fettucini, about 1⅓ (9-ounce) package, *Buitoni®*
3	tablespoons extra virgin olive oil, *Bertolli®*
¾	pound boneless skinless chicken breast, cut into bite-size pieces
1	package (8-ounce) sliced fresh brown mushrooms
1	teaspoon crushed garlic, *Christopher Ranch®*
2	teaspoons Italian seasoning, *McCormick®*
3	cups baby arugula, *Fresh Express®*
1	can (15-ounce) diced tomatoes with basil and oregano, *S&W®*
½	cup white wine
	Shredded Parmesan cheese, *DiGiorno®*

1. In a large pot of boiling salted water, cook pasta according to package instructions. Meanwhile, in a large skillet, heat oil over medium-high heat and add chicken, mushrooms, garlic, and Italian seasoning. Cook and stir until chicken is cooked through and mushrooms have released their juices, about 8 to 10 minutes.

2. Add arugula and cook and stir until wilted. Add tomatoes and wine. Bring to a boil, reduce heat, and simmer for 4 to 5 minutes. Drain pasta and toss with chicken mixture. Serve immediately with shredded Parmesan cheese.

Mixed Greens with Mandarin Oranges and Walnuts

Start to Finish 10 minutes
Makes 4 servings

1	can (4-ounce) mandarin orange segments, drained, juice reserved, *Geisha*
¼	cup olive oil vinaigrette, *Newman's Own*®
1	bag (5.5-ounce) mixed greens, *Fresh Express*®
1	can (5-ounce) hearts of palm, sliced
½	cucumber, sliced
¼	cup crumbled Gorgonzola cheese, *Bella*®
¼	cup chopped walnuts, *Diamond*®

1. Measure ¼ cup of reserved mandarin juice. In a small bowl, whisk together juice and vinaigrette. In a large bowl, toss together salad mix, hearts of palm, and mandarin segments with mandarin dressing.

2. Divide salad among 4 chilled plates. Compose salads with remaining ingredients.

Mozzarella Garlic Bread

Start to finish: 20 minutes
Makes 4 servings

1	(17-ounce) garlic bread in foil bag
2	cups shredded mozzarella, *Sargento*®
2	teaspoons Italian seasoning, *McCormick*®

1. Preheat oven to 400 degrees F. Line a baking sheet with aluminum foil. Remove garlic bread from foil bag.

2. Open bread and sprinkle each side with 1 cup mozzarella and 1 teaspoon Italian seasoning. Place on baking sheet and bake for 15 minutes or until cheese is bubbling and starting to brown slightly.

Fettucini with Lobster Sauce

Start to Finish 20 minutes
Makes 4 servings

Serving Ideas: For an elegant meal, drizzle with white truffle oil.

Haricots Verts with Shaved Parmesan (see below)

Pre-washed mesclun salad mix with champagne vinaigrette, *Girard's®*

A pink sauce plays up fettuccini's ribbony elegance, blending cream, sherry, shrimp bisque, and a lobster tail into a dish that's undeniably luxurious. Drizzle it with white truffle oil and serve with crispy haricots verts for a meal that's dinner-party worthy.

12	ounces refrigerated fettucini, about 1⅓ (9-ounce) packages, *Buitoni®*
1	can (10-ounce) condensed shrimp bisque, *Campbell's®*
½	cup half-and-half
¼	cup dry sherry, *Christian Brothers®*
1	cooked lobster tail, shelled

1. In a large pot of boiling salted water, cook fettucini according to package directions. In a medium saucepan, over medium heat, stir together bisque, half-and-half, and sherry. Bring to a boil, and reduce heat. Simmer for 5 minutes.

2. Slice lobster tail and add to sauce. Cook until heated through, about 2 to 3 minutes. Drain pasta and divide among four pasta bowls. Top with lobster sauce.

Haricots Verts with Shaved Parmesan

Start to Finish 10 minutes
Makes 4 servings

¾	pound ready-to-cook haricots verts, *Greenline®*
2	tablespoons sour cream
1	teaspoon lemon juice, *ReaLemon®*
¼	cup shaved parmesan, *DiGiorno®*
	Freshly ground black pepper

1. Place haricots verts in a large microwave-safe bowl. Cover and cook on HIGH for 5 to 7 minutes. Remove and drain, if necessary. In a small bowl, whisk together sour cream and lemon juice. Pour over haricots verts and toss to coat.

2. Serve immediately with shaved Parmesan and freshly ground pepper.

Linguine with Vegetable Alfredo

Start to Finish 20 minutes
Makes 4 servings

12	ounces refrigerated linguine, about 1⅓ (9-ounce) packages, *Buitoni*®
2	tablespoons extra virgin olive oil
1	package (5-ounce) diced tri-peppers, *Ready Pac*®
1	small zucchini, sliced
1	small yellow squash, sliced
1	cup frozen snap peas, thawed, *C&W*®
1	jar (16-ounce) creamy alfredo sauce, *Classico*®
1	tablespoon lemon juice, *ReaLemon*®
	Fresh parsley, chopped (optional)
	Grated Parmesan cheese, *DiGiorno*®

Serving Ideas:
Warm Spinach Salad with Eggs and Bacon (page 42)

Store-bought focaccia warmed in oven

1. In a large pot of boiling salted water, cook linguine according to package directions. In a large saucepan, heat olive oil over medium-high heat. Add peppers, zucchini, squash, and snap peas. Cook and stir until tender, about 5 minutes.

2. Stir in alfredo sauce, heat through, and fold in lemon juice. Add drained pasta to vegetable alfredo sauce, toss, and heat through. Garnish with chopped parsley (optional). Serve hot with grated Parmesan cheese.

Warm Spinach Salad with Eggs and Bacon

Start to Finish 10 minutes
Makes 4 servings

¼   cup olive oil and vinegar dressing, *Newman's Own*®
4   cups bagged baby spinach, *Ready Pac*®
1   cup quartered artichoke hearts, *Maria*®
2   hard-boiled eggs, peeled and sliced
¼   cup crumbled real bacon pieces, *Hormel*®

1. In a microwave-safe bowl, heat dressing in microwave on HIGH for 1½ to 2 minutes.

2. In a large bowl, combine spinach, artichoke hearts, eggs, and bacon. Pour warm dressing over top and toss to dress salad. Serve immediately.

Linguine with Zucchini Caponata

Start to Finish 20 minutes
Makes 4 servings

Slender linguine is often served with a seafood broth, but this vegetarian version is more substantial. Zucchini stands in for eggplant in a rustic stew-like sauce that begs for a hunk of bread for dipping. A Fresh Broccoli Salad makes a simple side.

Serving Ideas:
Fresh Broccoli Salad
(page 46)

Proscuitto-Wrapped
Breadsticks
(page 46)

12	ounces refrigerated linguine, about 1⅓ (9-ounce) packages, *Buitoni* ®
3	tablespoons extra virgin olive oil
½	cup ready-cut onion, *Ready Pac*®
½	cup frozen chopped green pepper, *Pictsweet*®
1	medium zucchini, diced
1	can (15-ounce) diced tomatoes with basil and oregano, *S&W*®
3	tablespoons capers, drained and rinsed
⅓	cup white wine
¼	cup balsamic vinegar
2	tablespoons light brown sugar
	Grated Parmesan cheese, *DiGiorno*®

1. In a large pot of boiling salted water, cook linguini according to package directions. In a large skillet, heat oil over medium-high heat, and add onion, green pepper, and zucchini. Cook and stir until vegetables are crisp-tender, about 8 to 10 minutes.

2. Add tomatoes, capers, wine, vinegar, and brown sugar. Bring to a boil, and reduce heat. Simmer for 5 minutes. Toss with cooked pasta. Serve hot with grated Parmesan cheese.

Fresh Broccoli Salad

Start to Finish 10 minutes
Makes 4 servings

4	cups cooked broccoli florets from grocery store salad bar
12	cherry tomatoes, cut in half
¼	cup red onion slivers, *Ready Pac®*
½	cup fresh pearl-size mozzarella, *Cantare®*
⅓	cup red wine vinaigrette, *Briana's®*
	Freshly ground black pepper

1. In a large bowl, toss together all ingredients, except black pepper.

2. Divide among 4 chilled salad plates. Serve with freshly ground pepper.

Prosciutto-Wrapped Breadsticks

Start to Finish 10 minutes
Makes 16 breadsticks

1	package (3-ounce) prosciutto
16	large breadsticks

1. Preheat oven to 400 degrees F. Line a baking sheet with foil. Separate slices of prosciutto. Slice each piece in half lengthwise.

2. Wind a half-slice of prosciutto around each breadstick and place on baking sheet. Bake for 5 to 7 minutes.

Angel Hair with Salmon in Lemon Cream Sauce

Start to Finish 20 minutes
Makes 4 servings

8	ounces dry angel hair pasta, *Barilla*®
1	pound fresh salmon, bones removed
	Salt and pepper
2	cans (6.5 ounces each) white sauce, *Aunt Penny's*®
6	tablespoons lemon juice, *ReaLemon*®
3	tablespoons capers
1	tablespoon Italian parsley, chopped
	Grated Parmesan cheese

Serving Ideas:
Garlicky Sautéed Green Beans and Peas (see below)

Warm baguette

Glass of white wine

1. In a large pot of boiling salted water, cook pasta according to package directions. Preheat broiler. Line a baking sheet with foil. Season salmon with salt and pepper and place on prepared baking sheet. Broil for 2 to 3 minutes per side. Remove and let cool to touch.

2. Meanwhile, in a large skillet, over medium-high heat, combine white sauce, lemon juice, and capers. Cook until smooth and heated through, about 2 minutes. Stir in parsley. Flake salmon into sauce. Drain pasta and divide among serving plates. Spoon sauce over pasta. Serve hot with grated Parmesan cheese.

Garlicky Sautéed Green Beans and Peas

Start to Finish 10 minutes
Makes 4 servings

2	tablespoons butter
1	garlic clove, minced
½	teaspoon salt-free citrus herb seasoning, *Spice Islands*®
1	cup frozen green beans, thawed, *C&W*®
1	cup frozen peas, thawed, *C&W*®
2	tablespoons diced pimientos, *Dromedary*®
	Salt and pepper

1. In a medium skillet, over medium-high heat, melt butter. Stir in garlic and citrus herb seasoning. Add green beans, peas, and pimientos.

2. Cook and stir for 3 to 5 minutes, or until heated through. Season with salt and pepper.

Penne Niçoise

Start to Finish 20 minutes
Makes 4 servings

Serving Ideas:
Arugula Salad
with Pears and
Gorgonzola
(see below)

Loaf of crusty French
bread with butter

In France, *à la niçoise* signifies a dish that hails from the coast of Nice. Typically served as a salad, this version ladles olive-oil-tossed vegetables, eggs, and tuna over penne pasta, with pears and gorgonzola topping a fragrant side salad.

8	ounces penne pasta (about half a box), *Barilla*®
1	cup olive oil and vinegar dressing, *Newman's Own*®
1½	cups precooked and diced seasoned potatoes, *Reser's*®
1	cup frozen haricots verts, thawed, *C&W*®
2	cans (6 ounces each) tuna in oil, drained, *Starkist*®
2	tablespoons capers
½	cup prepared olive bruschetta, *Delallo*®
3	hard-boiled eggs, peeled and sliced
	Grated Parmesan cheese, *DiGiorno*®

1. In a large pot of boiling salted water, cook penne according to package directions. In a large skillet, over medium-high heat, bring olive oil dressing to a boil. Reduce heat, and add potatoes and haricots verts. Cook for 1 minute. Add remaining ingredients and cook until heated through, about 2 to 3 minutes.

2. Toss cooked pasta with niçoise sauce; serve immediately with grated Parmesan cheese.

Arugula Salad with Pears and Gorgonzola

Start to Finish 10 minutes
Makes 4 servings

1	can (15-ounce) pear halves, drained and sliced, *Natural Style*, 2 tablespoons juice reserved, *S&W*®
2	tablespoons olive oil and vinegar dressing, *Newman's Own*®
	Salt and pepper
2	cups baby arugula
4	tablespoons Gorgonzola cheese, crumbled, *BelGioioso*®
4	tablespoons glazed pecans, *Emerald*®

1. In a large bowl, whisk together the reserved pear juice and olive oil and vinegar dressing. Season to taste with salt and pepper. Add arugula and toss to coat.

2. Divide dressed arugula among four chilled salad plates. Top each salad with 4 pear slices, Gorgonzola cheese, and pecans. Serve immediately.

Penne Puttanesca

Start to Finish 20 minutes
Makes 4 servings

8	ounces dry whole grain penne pasta (about ½ box), *Barilla Plus*®
1	jar (26-ounce) marinara sauce, *Barilla*®
1	teaspoon anchovies, chopped, *Reese*®
2	tablespoons capers
1	teaspoon crushed garlic, *Christopher Ranch*®
1	tablespoon Italian seasoning, *McCormick*®
½	teaspoon red pepper flakes, *McCormick*®
	Grated Parmesan cheese, *DiGiorno*®

Serving Ideas:
Zucchini al Formaggio
(see below)

Mixed salad greens
with balsamic
vinaigrette

1. In a large pot of boiling salted water, cook penne according to package directions. In a large saucepan, over medium-high heat, combine all remaining ingredients, except Parmesan cheese. Bring to a boil. Reduce heat and simmer.

2. Add drained pasta to puttanesca sauce and heat through. Serve hot with grated Parmesan cheese.

Zucchini al Formaggio

Start to Finish 10 minutes
Makes 4 servings

4	medium zucchini, sliced ¼-inch thick
4	tablespoons butter, melted
1	teaspoon Italian seasoning, *McCormick*®
¾	cup grated Parmesan cheese, *DiGiorno*®
2	tablespoons finely chopped fresh parsley
	Salt and pepper

1. Cook zucchini slices in a medium saucepan of lightly salted boiling water until tender, about 1 to 1½ minutes.

2. Remove to serving bowl with slotted spoon. Add remaining ingredients and toss to combine. Serve hot.

Bow Ties with Artichoke Pesto

Start to Finish 20 minutes
Makes 4 servings

Serving Ideas:
Balsamic Roasted
Tomatoes (page 57)

Caesar salad kit,
Fresh Express®

Fanciful farfalle—or butterfly pasta—enchants children and adults alike with its fluttery bow-tie shape. Topped with a basil-drenched artichoke pesto, it makes a summery pasta dish, with Balsamic Roasted Tomatoes as a colorful companion.

8	ounces bow tie pasta, (approximately half a box), *Barilla®*
2	jars (6.5 ounces each) marinated artichoke hearts, drained, *Mezzetta®*
¼	cup chopped walnuts, *Diamond®*
2	tablespoons grated Parmesan cheese, *DiGiorno®*
1	teaspoon lemon juice, *ReaLemon®*
3	tablespoons extra virgin olive oil
	Salt and pepper
2	tablespoons chopped fresh basil

1. In a large pot of boiling salted water, cook bow ties according to package directions. In food processor, combine artichoke hearts, walnuts, Parmesan cheese, and lemon juice. Process for 30 seconds. Slowly add in olive oil until mixture is a coarse paste. Transfer pesto to a large bowl. Season to taste with salt and pepper.

2. Drain pasta and add to pesto in bowl. Toss to coat. Stir in basil. Serve hot with grated Parmesan cheese.

Balsamic
Roasted Tomatoes

Start to Finish 10 minutes
Makes 4 servings

4	Roma tomatoes, halved
2	tablespoons light balsamic vinaigrette, *Newman's Own*®
3	teaspoons grated Parmesan cheese, *DiGiorno*®
1	tablespoon chopped fresh basil

1. Preheat oven to 400 degrees F. Line a baking sheet with foil. Place tomato halves on baking sheet and sprinkle with balsamic dressing and Parmesan cheese.

2. Top with chopped basil and roast for 10 to 12 minutes.

Orecchiette with Sweet Red Pepper Sauce

Start to Finish 20 minutes
Makes 4 servings

Serving Ideas:
Salad Bar Stir-Fry
(page 61)

Store-bought
garlic bread
heated in oven

Orecchiette translates to "little ears" and that's just what this artisan pasta resembles. Soft in the middle and chewier outside, the absorbent texture works well with thicker sauces, like a vegetable ragu.

12	ounces (about ¾ box) dry orecchiette pasta, *Barilla®*
⅓	cup extra virgin olive oil
1	large red onion, peeled and chopped
1	jar (15-ounce) roasted red peppers, drained and chopped, *Mezzetta®*
1	can (15-ounce) petite cut tomatoes with rich juice, *S&W®*
1½	teaspoons Italian seasoning, *McCormick®*
	Grated Parmesan cheese, *DiGiorno®*

1. In a large pot of boiling salted water, cook orecchiette according to package directions. In a large skillet, over medium heat, combine oil and onions. Cover and cook for 5 minutes. Stir in remaining ingredients, except Parmesan cheese. Bring to a boil. Reduce heat and simmer for 10 minutes.

2. Add cooked pasta to red pepper sauce and heat through. Serve hot with grated Parmesan cheese.

Salad Bar Stir-Fry

Start to Finish 20 minutes
Makes 4 servings

3	tablespoons extra virgin olive oil
1	teaspoon crushed garlic, *Christopher Ranch*®
1	pound favorite salad bar vegetables, your choice*
1	teaspoon dried thyme, *McCormick*®
2	tablespoons balsamic vinegar

1. In a large skillet, heat oil with garlic, over medium-high heat. Add vegetables and stir-fry for 5 to 8 minutes, or until they reach desired doneness.

2. Stir in thyme and vinegar. Serve immediately.

*NOTE If using broccoli or cauliflower florets, cover and cook in microwave on HIGH for 5 minutes.

Ravioli Balsamico

Start to Finish 10 minutes
Makes 4 servings

Serving Ideas:
Roasted Asparagus
with Portobello
Mushrooms
(see below)

Prewashed salad mix
with your favorite
vinaigrette

A loaf of crusty
sourdough bread

14	ounces refrigerated ravioli, four cheese, about 1½ (9-ounce) packages, *Buitoni®*
1¼	cups light balsamic vinaigrette, *Newman's Own®*
¼	cup julienne cut sun-dried tomatoes, chopped, *California®*
½	cup chopped walnuts, *Diamond®*
2	tablespoons butter, cold

1. In a large pot of boiling salted water, cook ravioli according to package directions. Meanwhile, in a large skillet, over medium-high heat, bring vinaigrette to a boil. Add sun-dried tomatoes and walnuts. Reduce heat and simmer for 2 to 3 minutes. Whisk in butter until sauce is smooth and shiny.

2. Drain pasta. Add to balsamic sauce and heat through.

Roasted Asparagus with Portobello Mushrooms

Start to Finish 20 minutes
Makes 4 servings

1	pound asparagus, trimmed and bottoms peeled
1	package (6-ounce) sliced portobello mushrooms, cut into 2-inch pieces
2	tablespoons extra virgin olive oil
½	teaspoon salt
¼	teaspoon ground black pepper
⅔	cup olive bruschetta topping, *Delallo®*

1. Preheat oven to 400 degrees F. Line a baking sheet with foil. Place asparagus and portobello mushrooms on prepared baking sheet. Drizzle with olive oil and season with salt and pepper. Sprinkle with bruschetta topping.

2. Roast for 10 to 15 minutes, or until asparagus reaches desired tenderness. Serve hot.

Ravioli with Marsala-Caper Sauce

Start to Finish 20 minutes
Makes 6 servings

2	packages (9 ounces each) refrigerated ravioli, chicken and roasted garlic, *Buitoni®*
1	can (14-ounce) low-sodium beef broth, *Swanson®*
¾	cup Marsala wine, *Paul Masson®*
2	packets (1.2 ounces each) brown gravy mix, *Knorr®*
2	tablespoons butter
2	tablespoons capers, drained and chopped
	Chopped fresh parsley (optional)
	Grated Parmesan cheese, *DiGiorno®*

Serving Ideas:
Sautéed Zucchini with Garlic and Herbs (see below)

Caesar salad kit, *Fresh Express®*

1. In a large pot of boiling salted water, cook ravioli according to package directions. In a medium saucepan, over medium-high heat, stir together beef broth, wine, gravy mix, butter, and capers. Bring to boil, stirring frequently. Reduce heat and simmer for 2 to 3 minutes.

2. Divide drained ravioli among serving plates. Spoon sauce over top and garnish with chopped parsley (optional). Serve hot with grated Parmesan cheese.

Sautéed Zucchini With Garlic and Herbs

Start to Finish 20 minutes
Makes 6 servings

2	tablespoons extra virgin olive oil
3	medium zucchini, sliced ¼ inch thick
2	scallions, chopped
1	teaspoon crushed garlic, *Christopher Ranch®*
⅔	cup vegetable broth, *Swanson®*
2	tablespoons garlic and herb sauce mix, *Knorr®*
2	tablespoons finely chopped flat leaf parsley
	Salt and pepper

1. In a large skillet, heat oil over medium-high heat. Add zucchini, scallions, and garlic. Cook and stir for 6 to 8 minutes, or until zucchini is tender.

2. Slowly pour in vegetable broth. Stir in sauce mix and parsley. Simmer for 1½ to 2 minutes. Season to taste with salt and pepper. Serve immediately.

Beef, Pork, and Lamb

I've always thought that preparing a meal is like arranging a bouquet—you put the showiest bloom in the center, then fill in all around it. For most of us, meat is our showiest dish, the centerpiece around which the rest of the meal is built. This chapter is filled with all kinds of meats, from beef to pork to lamb, paired with savory sides that make each meal blossom with taste and texture. Upgrade ho-hum ham sandwiches and chips to a divine Venetian Ham Panini and a Balsamic Melon Salad. Instead of old-fashioned pot roast, try trendy Pork Medallions with Creamy Pesto Sauce and Soft Goat Cheese Polenta. To make rib-eyes really sizzle, float them in a puddle of Cognac-Peppercorn Sauce and let Creamy Cheesy Potatoes and Broccoli stand in for a baked potato. Red meat or white, these meals are a cut above, so surround them with sides and serve with pride.

The Meals

Filet Mignon with Red Wine Mushrooms	69
Blue Cheese and Bacon Mashed Potatoes	70
Rib-Eye Steaks with Cognac-Peppercorn Sauce	73
Creamy Cheesy Potatoes and Broccoli	73
Steak House Salad with Horseradish Dressing	74
Beer Battered Onion Rings	77
Western Meatloaf Sandwich	78
Black Bean Salad	78
Pork Tenderloin with Apple-Jack Sauce	81
Maple Sweet Potatoes	82
Pork Medallions with Creamy Pesto Sauce	85
Soft Goat Cheese Polenta	86
Pork Piccata with Wilted Spinach	89
Fettuccine with Parmesan Sauce	90
Pork Loin Chops with Peach BBQ Sauce	93
Bourbon Creamed Corn	94
Carnitas Tacos	97
Green Chile Pintos	98
Venetian Ham Panini	101
Balsamic Melon Salad	101
Lamb Chops with Mango Chutney	102
Minted Broccoli Slaw	105
Lamb Chops with Garlic Yogurt Sauce	106
Glazed Carrots and Snap Peas with Golden Raisins	106
Lamb and Olive Skewers	109
Bulgur with Asparagus and Feta	110

Filet Mignon with
Red Wine Mushrooms

Start to Finish 20 minutes
Makes 4 servings

A stylish mushroom-Bordeaux sauce makes filet mignon effortlessly French. With a fine cut of beef, the side dishes can be simple. A little crumbled blue cheese, garlic, and bacon bits, and ready-made mashed potatoes are good to go.

Serving Ideas:
Blue Cheese and Bacon Mashed Potatoes (page 70)

Steamed frozen haricots verts

4	(6-ounce) beef filets*, rinsed and patted dry
2½	teaspoons Montreal steak seasoning, *McCormick*®
4	tablespoons butter
½	teaspoon crushed garlic, *Christopher Ranch*®
1	package (8-ounce) sliced brown mushrooms
½	cup frozen chopped onion, thawed, *Ore-Ida*®
½	cup red wine
1	cup low-sodium beef broth, *Swanson*®
1	packet (1-ounce) brown gravy mix, *Knorr*®

1. Preheat broiler. Line a heavy duty baking sheet with foil. Season filets with steak seasoning. Broil 6 to 8 inches from heat source for 5 minutes per side.

2. Meanwhile, in a large skillet over medium-high heat, melt butter and add garlic and mushrooms. Cook and stir for 8 to 10 minutes. Add onion, wine, and beef broth. Whisk in gravy mix and bring to a boil, stirring frequently. Reduce heat and simmer for 3 minutes, stirring occasionally. Serve filets hot with red wine mushrooms.

Note If filets are more than ½-inch thick, butterfly them horizontally.

Blue Cheese and Bacon Mashed Potatoes

Start to Finish 10 minutes
Makes 4 servings

1	container (24-ounce) mashed potatoes, *Country Crock Homestyle*®
½	cup crumbled blue cheese, *Treasure Cave*®
¼	teaspoon crushed garlic, *Christopher Ranch*®
2	tablespoons real crumbled bacon, *Hormel*®
¼	teaspoon Worcestershire sauce, *Lea & Perrins*®
	Butter (optional)

1. Heat mashed potatoes, uncovered, in microwave on HIGH for 5 minutes, stirring once halfway through cooking time. Transfer to a medium microwave-safe bowl.

2. Add remaining ingredients, except butter, and stir to combine. Heat in microwave on HIGH for another 2 minutes. If desired, stir in butter before serving.

Rib-Eye Steaks with Cognac-Peppercorn Sauce

Start to Finish 20 minutes
Makes 4 servings

4	rib-eye steaks
	Freshly ground black pepper
1	tablespoon au jus gravy mix, *Lawry's*®
1	cup low-sodium beef broth, *Swanson*®
¼	cup cognac
1	packet (1-ounce) peppercorn sauce mix, *Knorr*®

Serving Ideas:
Creamy Cheesy
Potatoes and Broccoli
(see below)

Salad mix with blue
cheese crumbles
and red wine
vinaigrette

1. Preheat broiler. Line a heavy duty baking sheet with foil. Season steaks with pepper and au jus mix. Place on prepared baking sheet and broil steaks 4 to 6 inches from heat source, for 5 minutes per side.

2. In a medium saucepan over medium-high heat, whisk together beef broth, cognac, and peppercorn sauce mix. Bring to a boil, stirring constantly. Reduce heat and simmer for 2 minutes. Drizzle hot steaks with cognac-peppercorn sauce.

Creamy Cheesy Potatoes and Broccoli

Start to Finish 10 minutes
Makes 4 servings

2	tablespoons extra virgin olive oil
1	package (16-ounce) precooked and diced red potatoes, *Reser's*®
1	teaspoon garlic salt, *Lawry's*®
1½	cups frozen chopped broccoli, thawed, *Birds Eye*®
1	can (10.5-ounce) white sauce, *Aunt Penny's*®
¾	cup finely shredded mild cheddar cheese, *Kraft*®

1. In a large skillet, heat oil over medium-high heat. Add potatoes and garlic salt. Cook and stir for 4 minutes. Stir in broccoli.

2. Reduce heat and stir in white sauce and cheese. Heat through, stirring often until cheese melts.

Steak House Salad
With Horseradish Dressing

Start to Finish 10 minutes
Makes 4 servings

Serving Ideas:
Beer Battered Onion
Rings (page 77)

A glass of cold beer

Leftover steak becomes a whole new dinner, sliced deli-style on a plate of garden greens and vegetables, and topped with a bold horseradish dressing. Team with easy Beer Battered Onion Rings and an ice-cold beer for an All-American meal.

¾	cup evaporated milk, *Carnation*®
¼	cup mayonnaise, *Best Foods*®
1	tablespoon lemon juice, *ReaLemon*®
1	tablespoon prepared horseradish, *Morehouse*®
1½	tablespoons finely chopped fresh chives
1	tablespoon finely chopped fresh flat leaf parsley
	Salt and pepper
12	ounces leftover cooked steak, sliced on the bias
1	bag (7-ounce) mixed greens, *Ready Pac*®
½	cucumber, sliced
1	tomato, sliced
1	cup croutons

1. In a medium bowl, whisk together milk, mayonnaise, lemon juice, horseradish, chives, and parsley. Season to taste with salt and pepper; set aside. Heat leftover steak in the microwave.

2. Divide mixed greens among 4 chilled dinner plates. Divide sliced cucumbers and tomatoes evenly among the salads. Top each salad with 3 ounces leftover steak. Pour dressing over each and top with ¼ cup of croutons.

Beer Battered Onion Rings

Start to Finish 20 minutes
Makes 4 servings

Peanut or vegetable oil
1   **sweet onion, peeled and sliced**
½   **cup flour**
2   **eggs**
1   **teaspoon celery salt**
2   **cups baking mix,** *Bisquick*®
1   **cup ale,** *Bass*®

1. In a Dutch oven, heat 4 inches of oil* over medium-high heat to 375 degrees F. In a shallow pan, dredge sliced onions in flour; set aside. In a large bowl, whisk together eggs and celery salt. Stir in baking mix and ale. (Batter will be lumpy.) Shake excess flour from onion slices and coat in batter.

2. When oil is ready, carefully slide battered onion slices into oil. Fry for 4 to 6 minutes, turning occasionally. Drain on paper towels. Serve immediately.

Western Meatloaf Sandwich

Start to Finish 10 minutes
Makes 4 servings

Serving Ideas:
Black Bean Salad
(see below)

A glass of cold beer

1   **package (17-ounce) prepared meatloaf, *Hormel*®**
2   **tablespoons tartar sauce, *Best Foods*®**
1   **tablespoon Dijon mustard, *Grey Poupon*®**
1   **tablespoon chili sauce, *Heinz*®**
4   **onion rolls**
4   **leaves romaine lettuce**
1   **tomato, sliced**
4   **slices pepper jack cheese, *Tillamook*®**
⅓   **cup french fried onions, *French's*®**

1. Cook meatloaf in microwave according to package directions, about 4 minutes. Remove from package, slice thick and set aside. Meanwhile, in a small bowl, stir together tartar sauce, mustard, and chili sauce.

2. Split onion rolls. Spread sauce on bottom half of rolls. Place lettuce and tomato slices on each. Top with a meatloaf slice, cheese slice, fried onions, and top half of roll. Serve immediately.

Black Bean Salad

Start to Finish 10 minutes
Makes 4 servings

1   **can (15-ounce) low-sodium black beans, drained and rinsed, *S&W*®**
¾   **cup premade pico de gallo, *Ready Pac*®**
½   **cup diced tri-peppers, *Ready Pack*®**
2   **tablespoons cilantro and pepita Caesar dressing, *El Torito*®**

1. In a large bowl, toss together all ingredients.

2. Serve immediately.

Pork Tenderloin with Apple-Jack Sauce

Start to Finish 20 minutes
Makes 4 servings

This pork tenderloin is served with a Southern whiskey-cider sauce that brings out the sweetness of the meat. The secret ingredient—mulling spices—plays off the Maple Sweet Potatoes to make your kitchen smell like a fresh-baked pie.

Serving Ideas:
Maple Sweet Potatoes (page 82)

Steamed frozen or fresh broccoli

⅓ cup flour
2 teaspoons Montreal chicken seasoning, *McCormick*®
1 teaspoon poultry seasoning, *McCormick*®
1¼ pounds pork tenderloin, sliced 1-inch thick
2 tablespoons extra virgin olive oil
½ cup whiskey, *Jack Daniels*®
¼ cup apple juice, frozen concentrate, thawed, *Tree Top*®
1 teaspoon Jamaican Jerk seasoning, *McCormick*®

1. Using a meat mallet, pound pork slices to ¼-inch thick and set aside. In a small bowl, combine flour, and chicken and poultry seasonings. Dredge pork slices with seasoned flour and shake off excess.

2. In a large skillet, heat oil, over medium-high heat. Sauté pork for 2 to 3 minutes per side or until golden. Remove pork from pan and set aside. Remove pan from heat and carefully add whiskey. Return pan to heat and scrape up brown bits from bottom of pan. Add juice concentrate and jerk seasoning. Bring to a boil and return meat to pan along with any accumulated juices. Bring to simmer. Cover pan, reduce heat to medium, and cook for 5 minutes. Serve hot.

Maple Sweet Potatoes

Start to Finish 10 minutes
Makes 4 servings

1	can (29-ounce) cut sweet potatoes, drained, *Princella®*
2	tablespoons butter
2	tablespoons pure maple syrup, *Spring Tree®*
½	teaspoon pumpkin pie spice, *McCormick®*
	Salt and pepper
	Chopped toasted pecans
	Additional pure maple syrup, *Spring Tree®*

1. Place drained sweet potatoes in a microwave-safe bowl. Cover and heat in microwave on HIGH for 5 minutes.

2. Remove and drain any liquid from bowl. Add all remaining ingredients. Use a fork and mash to combine. Season to taste with salt and pepper. Sprinkle with chopped toasted pecans and drizzle with additional maple syrup.

Pork Medallions with Creamy Pesto Sauce

Start to Finish 20 minutes
Makes 6 servings

1½	pounds pork tenderloin, sliced 1-inch thick
1	tablespoon plus 2 teaspoons Italian salad dressing mix, divided, *Good Seasons*®
	Flour
2	tablespoons extra virgin olive oil
1	can (10.5-ounce) white sauce, *Aunt Penny's*®
2	teaspoons lemon juice, *ReaLemon*®
1	container (7-ounce) premade pesto, *Buitoni*®

Serving Ideas:
Soft Goat Cheese Polenta (page 86)

Steamed frozen Italian vegetable medley

1. Using a meat mallet, pound tenderloin slices to ¼-inch thick. Season pork tenderloin with 1 tablespoon Italian salad dressing mix. Dredge in flour, shaking off excess.

2. In a large skillet, heat oil over medium-high heat and cook pork for 3 to 4 minutes per side or until done, working in batches if necessary. Remove from skillet and tent with foil; set aside in warm oven.

3. In a medium saucepan, over medium heat, heat white sauce. Stir in remaining 2 teaspoons of salad dressing mix, lemon juice, and pesto. Heat through and drizzle medallions with pesto sauce.

Soft Goat
Cheese Polenta

Start to Finish 10 minutes
Makes 6 servings

2	tablespoons butter
1	package (24-ounce) precooked polenta, *San Gennaro*®
1	cup half-and-half
4	ounces goat cheese, *Silver Goat*®
1	tablespoon finely chopped fresh tarragon
	Salt and pepper

1. In a medium saucepan, over medium heat, melt butter. Break polenta into small pieces and add to pan. Whisk in half-and-half and continue stirring until smooth and heated through.

2. Stir in cheese and tarragon. Heat until cheese is melted. Season to taste with salt and pepper.

Pork Piccata with Wilted Spinach

Start to Finish 20 minutes
Makes 4 servings

1 ¼ pounds scaloppini or thin-cut boneless pork chops
     Salt and pepper
¼   cup flour
1   tablespoon Italian seasoning, *McCormick®*
½   cup extra virgin olive oil
½   cup white wine
½   cup low-sodium chicken broth, *Swanson®*
4   tablespoons butter, divided
2   tablespoons capers, drained
1   bag (6-ounce) baby spinach, *Fresh Express®*

1. Season pork scallopini with salt and pepper. In a small bowl, stir together flour and Italian seasoning. Dredge pork in flour mixture and shake off excess.

2. In a large skillet, heat oil over medium-high heat. Sear pork for 3 to 4 minutes per side. Remove pork from pan and cover. Remove skillet from heat and carefully add white wine. Return skillet to heat and deglaze by scraping bits from bottom of pan. Reduce wine by half and add chicken broth. Bring to a boil. Whisk in 2 tablespoons of butter, 1 tablespoon at a time. Add capers.

3. Return pork and any accumulated juices to skillet. Cook until heated through, about 2 to 3 minutes. Transfer pork to a serving plate and drizzle with sauce. Wipe skillet clean with a paper towel. Return to heat and melt remaining 2 tablespoons of butter. Add spinach and cook and stir until just wilted, about 3 to 4 minutes.

Serving Ideas:
Fettuccine with Parmesan Sauce (page 90)

Caesar salad kit, *Fresh Express®*

Fettuccine with Parmesan Sauce

Start to Finish 10 minutes
Makes 4 servings

1	package (9-ounce) refrigerated fettuccine, *Buitoni®*
1	can (10.5-ounce) white sauce, *Aunt Penny's®*
⅓	cup grated Parmesan cheese, *DiGiorno®*
1	pinch cayenne pepper, *McCormick®*
1	tablespoon chopped flat leaf parsley

1. In a large pot of boiling salted water, cook fettuccine according to package directions. In a large microwave-safe bowl, heat white sauce in microwave on HIGH for 2 minutes, stirring once halfway through cooking time. Remove and stir in all remaining ingredients.

2. Drain pasta. Add to sauce and toss until well coated.

Pork Loin Chops
With Peach BBQ Sauce

Start to Finish 20 minutes
Makes 4 servings

4	boneless, thick-cut pork loin chops
4	teaspoons garlic salt, *Lawry's*
1	tablespoon canola oil
¼	cup frozen chopped onion, thawed, *Ore-Ida®*
2	teaspoons crushed garlic, *Christopher Ranch®*
1	bottle (12-ounce) chili sauce, *Heinz®*
1	can (8¼-ounce) sliced peaches, drained and chopped, juice reserved, *Del Monte Lite®*
1	tablespoon yellow mustard, *French's®*
2	tablespoons molasses, *Grandma's®*
1	tablespoon orange juice concentrate, *Minute Maid®*
1	tablespoon lemon juice, *ReaLemon®*
1	teaspoon Worcestershire sauce, *Lea & Perrins®*
¼	cup crumbled real bacon, *Hormel®*
	Salt and pepper

1. Preheat broiler. Line a heavy duty baking sheet with foil and set aside. Season both sides of pork chops with garlic salt. Place on prepared baking sheet. Broil 6 to 8 inches from heat source for 6 to 8 minutes per side.

2. In a medium saucepan, heat oil over medium-high heat. Add onions and garlic and cook and stir for 2 minutes. Add all remaining ingredients and bring to a boil. Reduce heat and simmer for 10 minutes. Serve pork chops drizzled with peach BBQ sauce.

Bourbon Creamed Corn

Start to Finish 10 minutes
Makes 4 servings

2	tablespoons bourbon, *Jim Beam*®
¼	cup heavy cream
2	tablespoons butter
1	can (11-ounce) mexicorn, drained, *Green Giant*®
½	cup frozen chopped onion, thawed, *Ore-Ida*®

1. In a small bowl, whisk together bourbon and heavy cream; set aside. In a large saucepan over medium-high heat, melt butter and add mexicorn and onion.

2. Cook and stir for 2 minutes. Stir in bourbon-cream mixture and heat through.

Carnitas Tacos

Start to Finish 10 minutes
Makes 4 servings

Seasoned roast pork flavored with onion and cilantro is satisfyingly thick and quick—ideal when you want supper in next to no time. For a change of pace, scoop the meat over Spanish rice, with Green Chile Pintos rounding out the meal.

Serving Ideas:
Green Chile Pintos
(page 98)

Spanish style rice,
*Uncle Ben's®
Ready Rice*

1	container (17-ounce) precooked pork roast, *Hormel®*
¼	cup enchilada sauce, *Las Palmas®*
1	teaspoon Mexican seasoning, *The Spice Hunter®*
8	(6-inch) white corn tortillas, *Mission®*
⅓	cup chopped onions, *Ready Pac®*
2	tablespoons chopped fresh cilantro
1	lime, cut into wedges
	Shredded lettuce
	Tomatoes, chopped, *Ready Pac®* (optional)

1. Remove pork roast from package and set aside. In a medium microwave-safe bowl, combine enchilada sauce and Mexican seasoning. Add pork roast. Cover with plastic wrap and heat in microwave on HIGH for 4 minutes; remove and set aside.

2. Place tortillas on a microwave-safe plate. Cover with moist paper towel and heat in microwave on HIGH for 1 minute. Meanwhile, use a fork to shred pork in bowl. Add onion and cilantro. Stir to combine. Divide pork mixture among heated tortillas. Serve tacos hot with lime wedges, lettuce, and tomatoes.

Green Chile Pintos

Start to Finish 10 minutes
Makes 4 servings

1	can (15-ounce) pinto beans, drained, *S&W*®
1	can (10-ounce) Mexican diced tomatoes, drained, *Rotel*®
1	can (4-ounce) diced green chiles, *Ortega*®
1	tablespoon tequila, *Jose Cuervo*®
2	teaspoons Mexican seasoning, *The Spice Hunter*®
½	cup Mexican cheese blend, *Sargento*®

1. In a medium saucepan, over medium-high heat, combine all ingredients, except cheese. Cook until heated through, about 4 minutes.

2. Add cheese and stir until melted.

Venetian Ham Panini

Start to Finish 10 minutes
Makes 4 servings

1	loaf ciabatta bread
1	package (10-ounce) deli sliced ham, *Hillshire Farm*®
¼	cup julienne cut sun-dried tomatoes, chopped, *California*®
4	teaspoons Italian seasoning, *McCormick*®
6	slices provolone cheese, *Sargento*®
8	fresh basil leaves

Serving Ideas:
Balsamic Melon Salad
(see below)

1. Preheat oven to 400 degrees F. Line a baking sheet with foil. Cut ciabatta loaf in half horizontally. Top bottom half of bread with ham slices, tomatoes, Italian seasoning, cheese, and basil leaves.

2. Assemble sandwich and place on prepared baking sheet. Bake until cheese is melted and sandwich is heated through, about 5 minutes. Cut panini into four portions and serve.

Balsamic Melon Salad

Start to Finish 10 minutes
Makes 4 servings

2	cups packaged melon medley, cut into bite-size pieces, *Ready Pac*®
2	teaspoons balsamic vinegar
1	tablespoon chopped fresh basil
1	teaspoon freshly ground black pepper

1. In a large bowl, toss together all ingredients.

2. Serve chilled or at room temperature.

Lamb Chops with Mango Chutney

Start to Finish 20 minutes
Makes 4 servings

Serving Ideas:
Minted Broccoli Slaw
(page 105)

Mediterranean Curry
Couscous, *Near East*®

Chunks of mango, red onion, and raisins give tender loin chops eye appeal, while cider-spiked chili powder adds a unique flavor blend. Minted Broccoli Slaw mixed with yogurt and honey ratchets up the sweet-hot laddering of tastes.

12	small lamb loin chops
1	tablespoon spicy Montreal steak seasoning, *McCormick Grill Mates*®
1	tablespoon canola oil
1	cup peeled and chopped red onion
2	cups frozen mango chunks, thawed and chopped, *Dole*®
½	cup golden raisins, *Sun-Maid*®
1	tablespoon apple cider vinegar, *Heinz*®
1	teaspoon chili powder, *Gebhardt's*®
1	teaspoon garam masala, *The Spice Hunter*®

1. Preheat broiler. Line a heavy duty baking sheet with foil. Season both sides of lamb chops with steak seasoning. Place on prepared baking sheet. Broil 6 to 8 inches from heat source for 4 minutes per side.

2. Meanwhile, in a medium saucepan, heat oil over medium heat. Add onion and cook and stir until soft, about 3 minutes. Add all remaining ingredients. Cook until heated through and cider vinegar has been absorbed. Remove lamb chops and let rest for 2 minutes. Serve lamb chops dolloped with mango chutney.

Minted Broccoli Slaw

Start to Finish 10 minutes
Makes 4 servings

1	medium cucumber, seeded
1	bag (12-ounce) broccoli coleslaw, *The Produce Stand*®
2	tablespoons finely chopped fresh mint
¾	cup Greek-style yogurt, *Pavel's*®
¼	cup honey, *Sue Bee*®
2	tablespoons apple cider vinegar, *Heinz*®

1. Grate cucumber into a large bowl. Add broccoli slaw and mint. Toss to combine thoroughly.

2. In a small bowl, whisk together yogurt, honey, and apple cider vinegar. Pour over slaw. Toss to mix thoroughly.

Lamb Chops with Garlic Yogurt Sauce

Start to Finish 10 minutes
Makes 4 servings

12	lamb rib chops, on bone, rinsed and patted dry
2	tablespoons Greek seasoning, *McCormick®*
¾	cup Greek-style yogurt, *Pavel's®*
1½	teaspoons garlic juice, *McCormick®*
3	teaspoons chopped fresh mint
	Salt and pepper

1. Preheat broiler. Line a heavy duty baking sheet with foil. Season both sides of lamb chops with Greek seasoning. Place on prepared baking sheet. Broil 6 to 8 inches from heat source for 4 to 5 minutes per side.

2. Meanwhile, in a small saucepan, over low heat, combine yogurt, garlic juice, and mint. Gently heat, stirring occasionally. (Do not heat too quickly or sauce will curdle.) Season sauce to taste with salt and pepper. Serve lamb chops immediately with sauce.

Serving Ideas:
Glazed Carrots and Snap Peas with Golden Raisins (see below)

Long grain rice seasoned with lemon juice and Greek seasoning, *Uncle Ben's® Ready Rice*

Glazed Carrots and Snap Peas with Golden Raisins

Start to Finish 10 minutes
Servings 4

2	cups frozen sliced carrots, *Birds Eye®*
2	cups frozen snap peas, *C&W®*
¼	cup honey, *Sue Bee®*
1	tablespoon lemon juice, *ReaLemon®*
1	teaspoon ground cinnamon, *McCormick®*
¼	cup golden raisins, *Sun Maid®*

1. In a microwave-safe bowl, combine carrots and snap peas. Cover and heat on HIGH for 5 minutes.

2. In a small bowl, combine honey, lemon juice, and cinnamon; set aside.

3. Remove vegetables from microwave. Stir in honey mixture and raisins. Re-cover and heat in microwave on HIGH for another 5 to 6 minuntes. Serve hot.

Lamb and Olive Skewers

Start to Finish 20 minutes
Makes 4 servings

Serving Ideas:
Rosemary skewers would be fantastic with these kabobs. Be sure to wrap exposed rosemary leaves with foil to keep from burning.

Bulgur with Asparagus and Feta (page 110)

Chopped romaine with olive oil vinaigrette, *Newman's Own®* and *Greek Seasoning®*

Lamb meatballs take on a festive air cooked on rosemary skewers that give the meat a subtle piney note. Briny olives and a side of Bulgur with Asparagus and Feta cleverly balance Mediterranean flavors in an earthy yet elegant combo.

1½	pounds lean lamb meat, cut in 1-inch cubes
2	tablespoons extra virgin olive oil
¼	cup chopped fresh flat leaf parsley
1	teaspoon garlic salt, *Lawry's®*
½	teaspoon ground black pepper
1	teaspoon garam masala, *The Spice Hunter®*
24	garlic stuffed green olives, *Santa Barbara®*
24	cherry tomatoes
4	pita pocket bread, *Sara Lee®*
	Store-bought tzatziki sauce

1. Soak wooden skewers in water for 30 minutes. Preheat broiler. Line a heavy duty baking sheet with foil. In a medium bowl, combine cubed lamb, oil, parsley, garlic salt, pepper, and garam marsala; mix thoroughly.

2. To make skewers, alternate lamb, olive, and tomatoes. Place skewers on prepared baking sheet. Broil 4 to 6 inches from heat source for 2 minutes per side for 8 to 10 total minutes. Serve skewers hot with pita bread and tzatziki sauce.

Bulgur with Asparagus and Feta

Start to Finish 20 minutes
Makes 4 servings

1	cup low-sodium chicken broth, *Swanson*®
¼	cup orange juice, *Minute Maid*®
1	cup bulgur, *Arrowhead Mills*®
1	box (10-ounce) frozen asparagus spears, *Birds Eye*®
1	teaspoon lemon zest
1	teaspoon extra virgin olive oil
2	tablespoons chopped pimientos, *Dromedary*®
1	package (4-ounce) crumbled feta cheese
	Salt and pepper

1. In a small saucepan, over medium-high heat, combine chicken broth, orange juice, and bulgur. Bring to a boil, stirring often. Cover, reduce heat, and simmer for 10 minutes.

2. Meanwhile, combine asparagus and lemon zest in a microwave-safe bowl. Cover and heat in microwave on HIGH for 5 to 6 minutes. Remove and drain any liquid. In a medium bowl, combine cooked bulgur, asparagus, and all remaining ingredients. Toss to combine. Season to taste with salt and pepper. Serve warm or at room temperature.

Fish and Shellfish

Where I grew up in Washington state, a thick, juicy steak was as likely to mean salmon or tuna as it was a filet mignon. I live near a different ocean now, but whenever I visit my sister and brothers in Seattle, we take the kids to Pike Place Market, where row after row of iced grouper and halibut, bins of rosy shrimp and clams, and tanks of lobsters and crabs are ours for the choosing. This chapter is like that, offering a little bit of everything so you can pick your favorites. Scallops and mushrooms balance earth and sea in a creamy chowder, trout expands the smoky taste of a BLT, and a tarragon-garlic rub gives an herbal lift to skewered shrimp. For special suppers, the clean citrusy taste of an orange-balsamic glaze brings out the flavor of salmon without taking flavor away—the secret to making any fish taste its best.

The Meals

Salmon with Chili-Lime Hollandaise	115
Mixed Greens Salad with Fingerlings and Bacon	116
Orange Balsamic Glazed Salmon	119
Mandarin Couscous	119
Swordfish with Ginger-Garlic Sauce	120
Siam Peanut Slaw	123
Wine Poached Tilapia with Herb Sauce	124
Green Beans with Brown Butter and Pine Nuts	124
Halibut with Champagne Mushroom Sauce	127
Herbed Rice Pilaf	128
Trout BLT	131
Creamy Red Potato Salad With Green Olives and Capers	132

Shrimp with Avocado in Tequila Cream Sauce	135
Jicama Slaw	135
Shrimp and Cheesy Grits	136
Spiced Zucchini	139
Tarragon Garlic Shrimp Skewers	140
Broccoli with Almond Brown Butter	143
Captain's Club with Shrimp and Chipotle Mayonnaise	144
Chilled Avocado Soup	147
Scallop and Mushroom Chowder	148
Spinach Salad with Mangos and Mandarins	151
Sicilian Steamers	152
Lemon Artichokes and Capers	155
Crab Parfait	156
Fiesta Tomato Soup	156

Quick Tip: To make the grilled fajita shrimp (see photo, upper left corner of page 112), marinate peeled and deveined raw shrimp in a mixture of 1 tablespoon fajita seasoning and 1 cup José Cuervo tequila for 10 minutes. Remove from marinade; discard. Grill shrimp for 2½ minutes or cook in a sauté pan. For an appetizer, serve shrimp on a toothpick; for a main dish, serve shrimp on a skewer.

Salmon with Chili-Lime Hollandaise

Start to Finish 10 minutes
Makes 4 servings

4	salmon steaks, 1-inch thick, rinsed and patted dry
4	teaspoons Mexican seasoning, divided, *The The Spice Hunter*®
1	cup milk
1	packet (0.9-ounce) Hollandaise sauce mix, *Knorr*®
¼	cup butter
1	tablespoon lime juice, *ReaLime*®
2	teaspoons chili powder, *Gebhardt's*®
	Pinch cayenne pepper
	Salt

Serving Ideas:
Mixed Greens Salad with Fingerlings and Bacon (page 116)

Frozen peas cooked with butter in microwave

1. Preheat broiler. Line a heavy duty baking sheet with foil. Season each salmon steak with one teaspoon of the Mexican seasoning. Place on prepared baking sheet. Broil for 4 to 5 minutes per side.

2. Meanwhile, in a medium saucepan, over medium-high heat, whisk together milk and Hollandaise sauce mix until smooth. Whisk in butter until melted. Cook for 1 minute, stirring constantly, until thickened. Remove from heat. Stir in lime juice, chili powder, and cayenne pepper. Season to taste with salt. Serve salmon steaks drizzled with warm Hollandaise.

Mixed Greens Salad with Fingerlings and Bacon

Start to Finish 10 minutes
Makes 4 servings

4 to 5	fingerling potatoes
¼	cup mayonnaise, *Best Foods®*
¼	cup olive oil and vinegar dressing, *Newman's Own®*
¼	cup real crumbled bacon, *Hormel®*
1	bag (5.5-ounce) mixed greens, *Fresh Express®*
2	Roma tomatoes, sliced
½	red onion, peeled and sliced
	Crumbled Gorgonzola cheese (optional)

1. Place fingerling potatoes in a microwave-safe dish. Cover and cook on HIGH heat in microwave for 5 to 6 minutes. Remove and let cool to touch. Meanwhile, in a large bowl, whisk together mayonnaise and olive oil dressing. Fold in bacon. Add salad mix and toss.

2. Divide dressed salad among four chilled salad plates. Cut each fingerling potato in half, lengthwise, and top each salad with 2 halves. Compose salads with the tomatoes, red onion, and cheese (optional).

Orange Balsamic Glazed Salmon

Start to Finish 10 minutes
Makes 4 servings

2	tablespoons orange juice concentrate, *Minute Maid*®
1	tablespoon ginger preserves, *Robertson's*®
1	tablespoon balsamic vinegar
4	salmon fillets, 1inch thick, bones removed, rinsed and patted dry
1	tablespoon plus 1 teaspoon salt-free citrus herb seasoning, *Spice Islands*®
1	orange, sliced

Serving Ideas:
Mandarin Couscous
(see below)

Steamed ready-to-cook broccoli florets, *Ready Pac*®

1. Preheat broiler. Line a baking sheet with foil and set aside. In small saucepan, over medium-high heat, combine orange juice concentrate, ginger preserves, and balsamic vinegar. Simmer until preserves melt, about 2 to 3 minutes. Remove from heat and set aside.

2. Meanwhile, season each salmon fillet with 1 teaspoon citrus herb seasoning. Place fillets on prepared baking sheet. Broil, skin side down, for 2 minutes. Turn and broil, skin side up, for 2 minutes. Return to skin side down and spoon glaze over each fillet. Top each with an orange slice and broil for 1 minute. Serve immediately.

Mandarin Couscous

Start to Finish 10 minutes
Makes 4 servings

1	cup low-sodium chicken broth, *Swanson*®
1	can (11-ounce) mandarin orange segments, drained, juice reserved, *Geisha*®
1	teaspoon chopped ginger, *Christopher Ranch*®
1	cup couscous, *Near East*®
1	tablespoon fresh, finely chopped parsley

1. In medium saucepan, over high heat, bring chicken broth, reserved mandarin orange juice, and chopped ginger to a boil.

2. Add couscous, cover, and remove from heat. Let sit for 5 minutes. Stir in orange segments and parsley.

Swordfish with Ginger-Garlic Sauce

Start to Finish 20 minutes
Makes 4 servings

Serving Ideas:
Siam Peanut Slaw
(page 123)

Long grain rice,
*Uncle Ben's®
Ready Rice*

Many cooks feel the meaty texture and rich taste of swordfish is best presented with just a splash of lemon and a sprinkle of pepper. I've found that an inspired pairing of more assertive flavors, like ginger and garlic, lets the fish's natural heartiness come into its own.

2	teaspoons Szechwan seasoning, *Spice Islands®*
1	teaspoon ground ginger, *McCormick®*
1¼	pounds swordfish steak, rinsed and patted dry
2	tablespoons canola oil
½	cup sake
½	cup ginger preserves, *Robertson's®*
2	teaspoons crushed garlic, *Christopher Ranch®*
¼	cup stir-fry sauce, *Kikkoman®*
2	tablespoons chili sauce, *Heinz®*

1. In a small bowl, stir together Szechwan seasoning and ground ginger. Season both sides of swordfish steaks with spice mixture and set aside. In a large skillet, heat oil over medium-high heat. Sear fish 4 to 5 minutes per side, or until cooked through. Remove from skillet, cover, and set aside.

2. Carefully add sake and deglaze by scraping brown bits from bottom of pan. Add preserves and stir until melted. Stir in remaining ingredients and bring to a boil. Return swordfish steaks and any accumulated juices to pan. Reduce heat and simmer for 4 to 5 minutes, or until heated through. Drizzle swordfish with ginger-garlic sauce.

Siam Peanut Slaw

Start to Finish 10 minutes
Makes 4 servings

¼ cup peanut sauce, *House of Tsang®*
1 tablespoon rice vinegar or white wine vinegar
3 cups shredded cabbage, *Fresh Express®*
1 cup bean sprouts
2 scallions, finely chopped
¼ cup chopped fresh cilantro
1 cup peanuts, *Planters®*

1. In a large bowl, whisk together peanut sauce and vinegar.

2. Add remaining ingredients. Toss to mix thoroughly. Serve immediately.

Wine Poached Tilapia with Herb Sauce

Start to Finish 20 minutes
Makes 6 servings

Serving Ideas:

Green Beans with Brown Butter and Pine Nuts (see below)

Caesar salad kit, *Fresh Express®*

Warm baguette

The firmer the flesh, the less moisture you want to take away, making poaching a wonderful choice for low-fat tilapia. A white wine sauce is simple yet sophisticated, with delicious, earthy, herbal undertones.

2	cups white wine
2	cups vegetable broth, *Swanson®*
1	rib celery, cut into 4 pieces
1	carrot, shaved and cut into 4 pieces
1	thick onion slice, peeled
6	tilapia fillets, rinsed and patted dry
2	teaspoons seafood seasoning, *Old Bay®*
1	packet (1.6-ounce) garlic herb sauce mix, *Knorr®*
1	tablespoon butter

1. In a large skillet, combine wine, vegetable broth, celery, carrot, and onion. Bring to a boil, and then reduce heat to a low simmer.

2. Season both sides of tilapia fillets with seafood seasoning. Carefully slide fillets into poaching liquid. Poach fillets for 8 to 10 minutes, or until cooked through. Remove fillets from skillet, cover, and set aside. Ladle 1½ cups poaching liquid into small saucepan. Stir in garlic herb sauce mix and butter. Bring to a boil. Reduce heat and simmer for 3 minutes. Serve tilapia hot with sauce drizzled over top.

Green Beans with Brown Butter and Pine Nuts

Start to Finish 10 minutes
Makes 6 servings

5	cups frozen petite green beans, *C&W®*
6	tablespoons butter
1	teaspoon crushed garlic, *Christopher Ranch®*
¼	cup pine nuts
	Salt and pepper

1. Place green beans with 2 tablespoons of water in a microwave-safe bowl. Cover and cook for 6 to 7 minutes. Meanwhile, melt butter in a large skillet over medium-high heat. As the butter bubbles it will start to turn brown and give off a nutty aroma. Once it has reached a light brown color, add garlic, pine nuts, and salt and pepper to taste. Cook and stir for 1 minute.

2. Add cooked and drained green beans. Toss to combine and heat through. Serve immediately.

Halibut with Champagne Mushroom Sauce

Start to Finish 20 minutes
Makes 4 servings

Halibut is often pan-fried with lemon and dill, but its delicate taste is enhanced by a sweeter sauce, like this silky champagne and mushroom sauté. Layer in color by nesting the fillet on a bed of greens, beside an Herbed Rice Pilaf.

1¼	pounds halibut fillets, rinsed and patted dry
1	tablespoon lemon juice, *ReaLemon*®
1	teaspoon lemon and herb seasoning, *McCormick*®
2	tablespoons butter
1	tablespoon olive oil
1	package (8-ounce) sliced fresh mushrooms
¾	cup extra dry champagne, *Korbel*®
⅓	cup condensed cream of mushroom soup, *Campbell's*®

1. Sprinkle halibut fillets with lemon juice and lemon and herb seasoning. In a large skillet, over medium-high heat, melt butter with oil. Sear halibut fillets for 4 to 5 minutes per side, or until just cooked through.

2. Remove fillets from pan. Add mushrooms and sauté for 5 minutes. Carefully add champagne and deglaze by scraping brown bits from bottom of pan. Stir in mushroom soup. Bring to a boil. Add fish and any accumulated juices to pan. Reduce heat and simmer for 2 to 3 minutes. Serve immediately with sauce.

Serving Ideas:
Herbed Rice Pilaf (page 128)

Frozen French-cut green beans cooked with butter in microwave

Spring salad mix with champagne vinaigrette, *Girard's*®

Herbed Rice Pilaf

Start to Finish 20 minutes
Makes 4 servings

1	tablespoon butter
1	tablespoon finely chopped celery
1	tablespoon finely chopped carrot
1	tablespoon peeled and finely chopped shallot
2	cups instant rice, uncooked, *Uncle Ben's*®
2	cups low-sodium chicken broth, *Swanson*®
2	tablespoons finely chopped fresh herbs (oregano, thyme, marjoram, etc.)

1. In a medium sauce pan, over medium-high heat, melt butter. Cook and stir vegetables until tender, about 5 minutes. Add rice and stir to combine. Add broth and bring to a boil.

2. Cover and remove from heat. Let sit for 5 minutes. Fluff rice with fork and stir in herbs. Serve hot.

Trout BLT

Nonstick cooking spray
½   cup mayonnaise, *Best Foods®*
1   tablespoon Dijon mustard, *Grey Poupon®*
1   teaspoon seafood seasoning, *Old Bay®*
4   boneless trout fillets, rinsed and patted dry
8   slices precooked bacon, *Farmer John® Quick Serve®*
4   sourdough sandwich rolls
4   leaves butter lettuce
2   tomatoes, sliced
1   medium red onion, peeled and sliced (optional)

Serving Ideas:
Creamy Red Potato
Salad (page 132)

Ice cold domestic beer

1. Preheat broiler and place rack 4 to 6 inches from heat source. Line a heavy duty baking sheet with foil, lightly coat with cooking spray, and set aside. In a small bowl, stir together mayonnaise, mustard, and seafood seasoning.

2. Place trout fillets, skin-side down, on prepared baking sheet. Spread each fillet with 1 teaspoon mayonnaise mixture. Broil for 2 minutes. Remove from oven and top each fillet with two strips of bacon. Broil for another minute.

3. Slice rolls in half horizontally. Spread with remaining mayonnaise mixture, to taste. Build each sandwich with lettuce, sliced tomato, and red onion (optional). Peel off trout skin prior to placing on top of bun. Use a spatula to place trout and bacon on sandwich.

Creamy Red Potato Salad with Green Olives and Capers

Start to Finish 10 minutes
Makes 4 servings

1	bag (16-ounce) precooked and diced red potatoes, *Reser's*®
2	tablespoons sliced green olives, *Early California*®
2	teaspoons capers
1	tablespoon chopped pimientos, *Dromedary*®
2	hard boiled eggs, peeled and chopped
1	rib celery, finely chopped
¼	cup finely chopped red onion
3	tablespoons mayonnaise, *Best Foods*®
1	teaspoon apple cider vinegar, *Heinz*®
1	teaspoon lemon and herb seasoning, *McCormick*®
2	tablespoons fresh chopped flat leaf parsley

1. Combine all ingredients in a large bowl.

2. Stir to combine. Serve immediately.

Shrimp with Avocado in Tequila Cream Sauce

Start to Finish Time 10 minutes
Makes 4 servings

Gulf shrimp, tequila, avocados, and chipotles blend the full-on flavors of Mexico into one irresistible entrée. The avocados bring out the shrimp's sweetness and the tequila punches up the flavor, with confetti-like Jicama Slaw enhancing eye appeal.

Serving Ideas:
Jicama Slaw
(see below)

Spanish-style rice,
Uncle Ben's Ready Rice®

Warm tortillas
with butter

2	tablespoons canola oil
1	pound medium shrimp, shelled and deveined
⅓	cup tequila, *Jose Cuervo®*
1	tablespoon butter
1	packet (1.6-ounce) garlic and herb sauce mix, *Knorr®*
1	canned chipotle chile in adobo sauce, chopped
1¼	cups milk
1	avocado, peeled, pitted, and cut into large chunks

1. In a large skillet, heat canola oil over medium-high heat. Sauté shrimp for 3 to 4 minutes, or until opaque. Remove from skillet and set aside. Pour tequila into skillet. Bring to a boil and cook off alcohol, about 1 minute.

2. Melt butter in skillet. Add garlic herb sauce mix, chipotle chile, and milk. Stir until sauce thickens and is heated through. Remove from heat and stir in cooked shrimp and avocado.

Jicama Slaw

Start to Finish 10 minutes
Makes 4 servings

1	medium jicama, peeled
2	cups angel hair coleslaw, *Fresh Express®*
1	can (11-ounce) mandarin orange segments, drained, ¼ cup juice reserved, *Geisha®*
1½	tablespoons fresh chopped cilantro
¼	cup mayonnaise, *Best Foods®*
3	tablespoons apple cider vinegar, *Heinz®*
¼	teaspoon chili powder, *Gebhardt's®*
½	teaspoon salt
¼	teaspoon ground black pepper

1. Use a grater to shred two cups of jicama into a large bowl. Add cole slaw, mandarin orange segments, and cilantro. In a small bowl, whisk together reserved mandarin juice, mayonnaise, vinegar, chili powder, salt, and pepper.

2. Pour dressing over jicama mixture. Toss to mix thoroughly. Serve immediately.

Shrimp and Cheesy Grits

Start to Finish 20 minutes
Makes 4 servings

Serving Ideas:
Spiced Zucchini
(page 139)

Packaged romaine
hearts with cilantro-
pepita salad dressing,
El Torito®

FOR GRITS
3¾ **cups milk**
2 **tablespoons butter**
1 **cup frozen seasoned vegetable blend, *Pictsweet*®**
1 **cup shredded cheddar cheese, *Kraft*®**
4 **envelopes (1.0 ounce each) instant grits, *Quaker Oats*®**

FOR SHRIMP
2 **tablespoons olive oil, *Bertolli***
1 **teaspoon crushed garlic, *Christopher Ranch*®**
⅓ **cup crumbled real bacon, *Hormel*®**
1 **pound medium shrimp, shelled and deveined**
   hot sauce, *Tabasco*® (optional)

1. For grits, bring milk, butter, and seasoning blend to a boil in a medium saucepan over high heat. Remove from heat and stir in cheese and grits; set aside.

2. For the shrimp, heat oil with garlic and bacon in a large skillet, over medium-high heat. Add shrimp and sauté for 3 to 4 minutes, or until opaque. Serve shrimp hot over cheesy grits with Tabasco sauce (optional).

Spiced Zucchini

Start to Finish 10 minutes
Makes 4 servings

2	tablespoons extra virgin olive oil, *Bertolli*®
1	teaspoon crushed garlic, *Christopher Ranch*®
2	medium zucchini, sliced 1/4-inch thick
1	can (15-ounce) petite diced tomatoes, *S&W*®
1	cup frozen seasoned vegetables blend, *Pictsweet*®
½	teaspoon ground cinnamon, *McCormick*®
¼	teaspoon cayenne pepper, *McCormick*®
¼	cup fresh finely chopped cilantro
	Salt and black pepper

1. In a large skillet, heat oil and garlic over medium-high heat. Add zucchini and sauté for 5 to 6 minutes. Add tomatoes, seasoned vegetable blend, cinnamon, and cayenne pepper. Bring to a boil.

2. Reduce heat and simmer for 2 to 3 minutes. Stir in cilantro. Season to taste with salt and black pepper. Serve hot.

Tarragon Garlic Shrimp Skewers

Start to Finish 20 minutes
Makes 4 servings

Serving Ideas:
Broccoli with
Almond Brown Butter
(page 143)

Long grain wild rice,
Uncle Ben's®
Ready Rice

1	pound medium (24 count) shrimp, shelled and deveined
2	teaspoons salt-free lemon pepper seasoning, *McCormick®*
12	cherry tomatoes
⅓	cup butter
2	tablespoons fresh chopped tarragon
1½	teaspoons crushed garlic, *Christopher Ranch®*

1. Preheat broiler. Soak wooden skewers in water for 30 minutes. Line a heavy duty baking sheet with foil. In a medium bowl, season shrimp with lemon pepper seasoning. Toss to coat. Skewer three cherry tomatoes between three shrimp and repeat to make eight skewers.

2. Place skewers on prepared baking sheet. Broil for 1 to 2 minutes per side.

3. In a small sauce pan over medium heat, melt butter. Stir in tarragon and garlic. Remove from heat. Serve shrimp skewers hot with a drizzle of tarragon butter over top.

Broccoli with Almond Brown Butter

Start to Finish 10 minutes
Makes 4 servings

2	cups broccoli florets
2	tablespoons water
¼	cup butter
½	cup sliced almonds, *Planters*®
¼	cup french fried onions, *French's*®

1. Place broccoli florets and water in a large microwave-safe bowl. Cover and heat on HIGH in microwave for 2 minutes. Remove and drain any liquid.

2. In a medium skillet over medium-high heat, melt butter. Cook until golden brown, swirling pan often to prevent burning. Stir in almonds. Remove from heat. Pour browned butter over broccoli in bowl. Add french fried onions. Toss to combine. Serve immediately.

Captain's Club with Shrimp and Chipotle Mayonnaise

Start to Finish 10 minutes
Makes 4 sandwiches

Serving Ideas:
Chilled Avocado Soup
(page 147)

8	slices precooked bacon, *Farmer John® Quick Serve®*
1	pound cooked bay shrimp
2	ribs celery, diced
½	cup chipotle mayonnaise, *Best Foods®*
1	tablespoon lime juice, *ReaLime®*
1	tablespoon fresh chopped cilantro
	salt and pepper
12	slices sourdough bread, toasted
2	tomatoes, sliced
1	avocado, pitted, peeled, and sliced

1. Place bacon on a microwave-safe plate. Heat on HIGH in microwave for 40 to 60 seconds. In a medium bowl, combine shrimp, celery, mayonnaise, lime juice, and cilantro. Mix thoroughly. Season to taste with salt and pepper.

2. To assemble, top one slice of toasted bread with ¼ cup of shrimp mixture and three tomato slices. Place another slice of bread on top. Add ¼ cup more of shrimp mixture, two slices avocado, and two slices bacon. Top with another slice of toasted bread. Repeat with remaining ingredients to make three more sandwiches. Cut sandwiches in half diagonally to serve.

Chilled Avocado Soup

Start to Finish 20 minutes
Makes 4 servings

1½	cups vegetable broth, *Swanson*®
2	containers (12 ounces each) premade guacamole, *Calavo*®
1	can (4-ounce) diced green chiles, *Ortega*®
2	tablespoons lemon juice, *ReaLemon*®
2	tablespoons garlic salt, *Lawry's*®
2	tablespoons fresh chopped cilantro
4	tablespoons premade salsa
4	tablespoons sour cream
	Mild jalapeño *Tabasco*® (optional)

1. Combine all ingredients, except salsa and sour cream, in a blender. Blend until smooth. Chill in freezer for 15 minutes.

2. Divide among four serving bowls. Top each with one tablespoon salsa and one tablespoon sour cream. Serve with mild jalapeño Tabasco® (optional).

Scallop and Mushroom Chowder

Start to Finish 20 minutes
Makes 4 servings

Serving Ideas:
Spinach Salad
with Mangos and
Mandarins (page 151)

Loaf of crusty bread

Glass of white wine

4   tablespoons butter, divided
½   pound bay scallops, rinsed and patted dry
¼   cup flour
1   package (8-ounce) sliced mushrooms
1   rib celery, finely chopped
1   bottle (8-ounce) clam juice, *Snow's*®
¼   cup white wine, Chardonnay
1   can (10-ounce) condensed cream of potato soup, *Campbell's*®
1   teaspoon seafood seasoning, *Old Bay*®
1   cup precooked and diced red potatoes, *Reser's*®
½   cup cream
     Fresh chopped parsley (optional)

1. In a medium pot over medium-high heat, melt 2 tablespoons butter. Dredge scallops in flour. Shake off excess and sauté in butter for 3 to 4 minutes, or until opaque and starting to color. Use a slotted spoon to remove scallops from pan and set aside.

2. Melt remaining 2 tablespoons of butter in pot. Sauté mushrooms and celery for 5 minutes. Stir in clam juice, wine, potato soup, and seafood seasoning. Add potatoes and bring to boil. Reduce heat and stir in scallops with any accumulated juice. Simmer for 5 minutes. Remove from heat and stir in cream. Serve chowder hot, garnished with chopped parsley (optional).

Spinach Salad with Mangos and Mandarins

Start to Finish 10 minutes
Makes 4 servings

1	can (15-ounce) mandarin orange segments, drained, juice reserved, *Geisha*®
⅓	cup mayonnaise, *Best Foods*®
1	teaspoon poppy seeds, *McCormick*®
2	teaspoons lemon juice, *ReaLemon*®
8	cups bagged baby spinach, *Fresh Express*®
1⅓	cups mango slices, diced, *Harvest*®
⅓	cup red onion slivers, *Ready Pac*®
2	tablespoons slivered almonds, *Planters*®

1. Measure ⅓ cup of reserved mandarin juice. In a medium bowl, whisk together mandarin juice, mayonnaise, poppy seeds, and lemon juice.

2. Divide spinach among four chilled salad plates. Compose salads with remaining ingredients. Serve salads drizzled with mandarin dressing.

Sicilian Steamers

Start to Finish 20 minutes
Makes 4 servings

Serving Ideas:

Lemon Artichokes with Capers (page 155)

Crusty bread for soaking up broth

Littleneck clams are traditionally served New England-style in their own buttery broth, but the flavors of Sicily notch up the impact. Red peppers and pesto harmonize in a heat that's superbly counterbalanced by lemony artichokes.

4	pounds fresh, live littleneck clams, scrubbed
	Water
	Kosher salt
	Cornmeal
½	cup butter
3	bottles (8 ounces each) clam juice, *Snow's*®
1	cup white wine
1	tablespoon salt-free seafood grill and broiler, *The Spice Hunter*®
1	teaspoon red pepper flakes
1	tablespoon crushed garlic, *Christopher Ranch*®
1	can (15-ounce) petite diced tomatoes, *Hunt's*®
1	packet (0.5-ounce) pesto sauce mix, *Knorr*®
1	package (9-ounce) fresh linguine, cooked according to package directions, *Buitoni*®

1. At least 1 hour before cooking, soak clams in one gallon of water with ⅓ cup kosher salt and 1 cup cornmeal. (Do not use iodized salt as it will instantly kill the clams.) Keep refrigerated.

2. In a steamer or a large pot, add all ingredients except clams and linguine. Bring to boil. Reduce heat to a low boil and add clams. Cover with a tight-fitting lid and steam over low heat until clams have opened, about 5 to 10 minutes. Discard any clams that have not opened.

3. Divide cooked linguine and opened clams among four warmed pasta bowls. Ladle broth over the top. Serve immediately.

Lemon Artichokes with Capers

Start to Finish 10 minutes
Makes 4 servings

2	cans (15 ounces each) artichoke quarters, drained, *Maria*®
4	tablespoons butter
2	tablespoons lemon juice, *ReaLemon*®
2	tablespoons capers
2	tablespoons chopped fresh parsley

1. Place artichoke quarters in a microwave-safe bowl. Cover and cook on HIGH in microwave for 2 to 3 minutes.

2. In a medium skillet over medium-high heat, melt butter. Add cooked artichokes, lemon juice, and capers. Heat through, spooning sauce over artichokes. Stir in parsley. Serve hot.

Crab Parfait

Start to Finish 10 minutes
Makes 4 servings

Serving Ideas:

Fiesta Tomato Soup
(see below)

Warm tortillas
with butter

Margarita or cold
Mexican beer

Crab is thought of as "fancy food," so why not play up the presentation by layering it with vibrant guacamole and pico de gallo in a pretty parfait glass. Pair it with Fiesta Tomato Soup to make a refined light meal for guests.

2	cups shredded lettuce, *Ready Pac*®
¾	cup premade pico de gallo, divided, *Ready Pac*®
1	cup lump crabmeat, *Crown Prince*®
¼	cup premade guacamole, *Calavo*®
¼	cup sour cream
	Lemon, sliced (optional)

1. In each parfait or large wine glass, layer ½ cup shredded lettuce, 2 tablespoons pico de gallo, ¼ cup crabmeat, 1 tablespoon guacamole, and 1 tablespoon sour cream.

2. Top with 1 tablespoon pico de gallo and serve topped with lemon slices (optional).

Fiesta Tomato Soup

Start to Finish 10 minutes
Makes 4 servings

1	can (10¾-ounce) condensed tomato soup, *Campbell's*®
¼	cup tequila, *Jose Cuervo*®
¾	cup water
1	cup mexicorn, *Green Giant*®
1	can (4-ounce) diced green chiles, *Ortega*®
¼	teaspoon Tabasco® sauce
½	teaspoon lime juice, *ReaLime*®
1	tablespoon chopped fresh cilantro
	Limes, sliced

1. In a medium saucepan, over high heat, combine tomato soup, tequila, and water. Bring to a boil. Stir in mexicorn, green chiles, Tabasco®, and lime juice.

2. Reduce heat and simmer for 2 to 3 minutes. Remove from heat and stir in cilantro. Serve soup hot with lime slices.

Chicken and Turkey

It was called **assiette de poulet**—plateful of chicken—and I ordered it at a charming little French café in West Hollywood. A plump chicken breast, thigh, and wing filled the plate, with a dumpling stuffed with chicken pâté served in a bowl of chicken broth on the side. It was sublime proof of what my Grandma Dicie said all along: There are endless ways to fix chicken and every piece is good. Soup, salad, sandwich, or entrée, this chapter celebrates poultry in all its glory. Serve BBQ chicken atop mixed greens and serve it with Chile and Cheddar Corn Muffins. Smother chicken and mushrooms in creamy tarragon sauce to make it soothingly soupy. Top turkey with Madeira-laced portobellos and it's dressed for guests. If you have leftovers, you're lucky—they make a delightful sandwich for lunch the next day.

The Meals

Chicken with Lemon-Thyme Brown Butter	161
Warm Orzo Salad with Peas, Mint, and Feta	162
Orange-Walnut Pesto Chicken	165
Ranch Mashed Potatoes	165
Chicken with Peach and Melon Salsa	166
Black Bean and Spinach Couscous	169
Wasabi Chicken	170
Four Pea Stir-Fry	173
Chicken and Mushrooms in Creamy Tarragon Sauce	174
Nutty Herbed Rice	174
Chicken Vera Cruz	177
Cilantro-Garlic Potatoes	178

Pesto Chicken Panini	181
Tuscan Tomato Soup with Basil	182
Bourbon Chicken Sandwich	185
Peach Tree Slaw	186
BBQ Chicken Salad	189
Chile and Cheddar Corn Muffins	189
Turkey with Portobello Sauce	190
Spinach and Tomatoes with Feta	193
Turkey Cutlets with Cranberry Chutney	194
Roasted Asparagus with Lemony Hollandaise	197
Olympic Hero	198
Greek Garlic Fries	201
Tunisian Turkey Salad	202
Curried Apple Squash Soup	205

Chicken with Lemon-Thyme Brown Butter

Start to Finish 20 minutes
Makes 4 servings

1 ¼	pounds boneless, skinless chicken breast, thin-cut fillets, rinsed and patted dry
	Salt and pepper
2	teaspoons Italian seasoning, *McCormick*®
2	tablespoons extra virgin olive oil
1	stick (½ cup) butter
2	teaspoons fresh chopped thyme leaves
2	tablespoons lemon juice, *ReaLemon*®

Serving Ideas:
Warm Orzo Salad with Peas, Mint, and Feta (page 162)

Caesar salad kit, *Fresh Express*®

1. Season both sides of chicken breasts with salt, pepper, and Italian seasoning; set aside. Heat oil in a large skillet over medium-high heat. Add chicken breasts and sauté for 3 to 4 minutes per side, or until cooked through. Remove chicken from skillet and set aside.

2. Melt butter in skillet. When butter starts to foam and turn brown, remove from heat. Carefully stir in thyme and lemon juice as juice will splatter. Return pan to heat. Add chicken and any accumulated juices. Heat chicken through, turning to coat with sauce. Serve immediately, drizzled with a small amount of sauce.

Warm Orzo Salad
with Peas, Mint, and Feta

8	ounces (approximately ½ box) orzo, *Barilla®*
2	cups frozen early peas, *S&W®*
¼	cup olive oil and vinegar dressing, *Newman's Own®*
1	tablespoon lemon juice, *ReaLemon®*
¼	cup fresh chopped mint leaves
1	package (4-ounce) garlic and herb crumbled feta, *Athenos®*

1. In a large pot of boiling salted water, cook orzo according to package directions. When orzo is al dente, remove pot from heat and add frozen peas to orzo in the cooking water. Let sit for 1 minute. Drain and transfer to a serving bowl.

2. Stir in remaining ingredients. Serve warm.

Orange-Walnut Pesto Chicken

Start to Finish 20 minutes
Makes 4 servings

Fried chicken and mashed potatoes are classic comfort food. Take a more trendy—and healthful—approach by blending premade pesto, walnuts, and orange juice into a piquant crust and dishing up ranch dressing-flavored mashed potatoes alongside.

Serving Ideas:
Ranch Mashed Potatoes (see below)

Baby spinach, *Fresh Express®*, sautéed in olive oil and garlic,

4	boneless, skinless chicken breasts, rinsed and patted dry
	Salt and pepper
1	container (8-ounce) premade pesto, *Buitoni®*
1	cup chopped walnuts, *Diamond®*
¼	cup orange juice, *Minute Maid®*

1. Preheat broiler and place rack 4 to 6 inches from heat source. Line a heavy duty baking sheet with foil. Season chicken breasts with salt and pepper. Place on prepared baking sheet. Broil chicken breasts for 4 to 5 minutes per side, or until cooked through.

2. Meanwhile, in a blender, combine pesto, walnuts, and orange juice. Puree to a smooth consistency. Spoon orange-walnut pesto over chicken breasts and spread evenly. Return chicken to broiler and broil for 1 to 2 minutes. Remove and serve immediately.

Ranch Mashed Potatoes

Start to Finish 10 minutes
Makes 4 servings

1	container (24-ounce) mashed potatoes, *Country Crock Homestyle®*
1	packet (1.0-ounce) ranch seasoning and salad dressing mix, *Hidden Valley®*
¼	cup sour cream
½	teaspoon crushed garlic, *Christopher Ranch®*

1. Heat mashed potatoes, uncovered, in microwave on HIGH for 3 minutes. Transfer to a medium microwave-safe bowl.

2. Add remaining ingredients and stir to combine. Heat in microwave on HIGH for another 2 to 3 minutes. Stir before serving.

Chicken with Peach and Melon Salsa

Start to Finish 20 minutes
Makes 4 servings

Serving Ideas:
Black Bean and
Spinach Couscous
(page 169)

Spring mix salad,
Fresh Express®, with
red wine vinaigrette,

4	boneless, skinless chicken breasts, rinsed and patted dry
4	teaspoons Jamaican Jerk seasoning, *The Spice Hunter*®
1	can (15-ounce) peach slices, drained and diced, *Del Monte*®
1	cup precut melon medley, diced, *Ready Pac*®
1	tablespoon diced pimientos, *Dromedary*®
1	tablespoon fresh chopped cilantro
1	tablespoon lime juice, *ReaLime*®
½	teaspoon salt

1. Heat a grill pan over medium-high heat. Season both sides of each chicken breast with one teaspoon Jamaican Jerk seasoning. Place chicken breasts in pan and grill for 4 to 5 minutes per side, or until cooked through.

2. Meanwhile, in a medium bowl, combine remaining ingredients and stir thoroughly. Serve chicken topped with peach and melon salsa.

Black Bean and Spinach Couscous

Start to Finish 10 minutes
Makes 4 servings

1½ cups low-sodium chicken broth, *Swanson*®
1 cup couscous, *Near East*®
1 package (10-ounce) frozen chopped spinach, thawed, *Birds Eye*®
¾ cup black beans, drained, *S&W*®
2 teaspoons lemon juice, *ReaLemon*®
   Salt and pepper

1. In a medium saucepan over high heat, bring chicken broth to a boil. Remove from heat and stir in couscous. Cover and let sit for 5 minutes.

2. Squeeze excess water out of thawed spinach. In a microwave-safe bowl, combine spinach and black beans. Heat in microwave on HIGH for 2 minutes. Stir spinach and black bean mixture into couscous. Add lemon juice and season to taste with salt and pepper.

Wasabi Chicken

Start to Finish 20 minutes
Makes 4 servings

Serving Ideas:
Four Pea Stir Fry
(page 173)

Long grain rice,
Uncle Ben's®
Ready Rice

Fiery wasabi is Japanese horseradish. Tempered with ginger, its tangy hot mustard taste adds spark to mellow chicken breasts. Serve it with Four Pea Stir-Fry to deliver the signature flavors of Asian cooking—sweet, sour, spicy, and salty.

2	teaspoons wasabi powder, *Eden®*
1	tablespoon hot water
1	tablespoon canola oil
1	teaspoon minced ginger, *Christopher Ranch®*
4	boneless, skinless thin-cut chicken fillets, rinsed and patted dry
½	cup sake, *Gekkeikan®*
1	can (10.5-ounce) white sauce, *Aunt Penny's®*

1. In a small bowl, combine wasabi powder and hot water. Let sit for 5 minutes to make a paste. Meanwhile, in a large skillet, heat oil and ginger over medium-high heat. Add chicken and cook 3 to 4 minutes per side, or until cooked through. Remove chicken from skillet.

2. Remove skillet from heat and carefully add sake. Deglaze by scraping bits from bottom of pan. Return skillet to heat and add wasabi paste; stir and heat until dissolved. Stir in white sauce and heat through. Return chicken to pan and heat through. Serve chicken immediately with wasabi sauce.

Four Pea Stir-Fry

Start to Finish 10 minutes
Makes 4 servings

1	tablespoon canola oil
1	teaspoon sesame seed oil
1	teaspoon crushed garlic, *Christopher Ranch*®
1	cup prewashed snow peas, thawed, *C&W*®
1	cup frozen sugar snaps, thawed
1	cup frozen early peas, thawed, *C&W*®
¼	cup wasabi peas, lightly crushed, *Hapi*®
1	tablespoon diced pimientos, *Dromedary*®
2	tablespoons stir-fry sauce, *Kikkoman*®

1. In a large skillet, heat canola oil and sesame seed oil over medium-high heat.

2. Stir in garlic. Add all peas and pimientos. Cook and stir until peas and pimientos are tender, about 5 minutes. Stir in stir-fry sauce and serve.

Chicken and Mushrooms in Creamy Tarragon Sauce

Start to Finish 20 minutes
Makes 4 servings

Serving Ideas:
Nutty Herbed Rice
(see below)

Steamed green
vegetable

2	tablespoons extra virgin olive oil
1½	pounds boneless, skinless chicken breasts, cut into bite-size pieces
1	package (8-ounce) fresh sliced mushrooms
1	teaspoon salt-free lemon pepper, *McCormick*®
1	teaspoon crushed garlic, *Christopher Ranch*®
1	can (10-ounce) condensed cream of mushroom soup, *Campbell's*®
½	cup white wine, Chardonnay
3	tablespoons fresh chopped tarragon

1. In a large skillet, heat oil over medium-high heat. Add chicken and mushrooms. Cook and stir until chicken is cooked through, about 8 to 10 minutes.

2. Add remaining ingredients and stir thoroughly. Bring to a boil. Reduce heat and simmer for 5 minutes. Serve hot.

Nutty Herbed Rice

Start to Finish 10 minutes
Makes 4 servings

2	packages (8.8 ounces each) whole grain brown *Uncle Ben's*® *Ready Rice*
2	tablespoons butter
⅓	cup chopped nut topping, *Diamond*®
¼	cup fresh chopped herbs (parsley, thyme, marjoram, etc.)

1. Heat rice in microwave per package directions.

2. In a medium skillet, over medium-high heat, melt butter. Add nuts and toast for 30 seconds. Stir in rice and herbs. Serve immediately.

Chicken Vera Cruz

Start to Finish 20 minutes
Makes 4 servings

Chunked chicken breasts go Cal-Mex with a Mediterranean medley of tomatoes, olives, and fresh cilantro tossed in olive oil and garlic. Team it with a side of Cilantro-Garlic Potatoes, flavor-boosted with bacon, to round out the bold fiesta flavors.

Serving Ideas:
Cilantro-Garlic Potatoes
(page 178)

Sautéed okra with
lime juice

2	tablespoons extra virgin olive oil
1½	pounds boneless, skinless chicken breasts, cut into bite-size pieces
1½	teaspoons Mexican seasoning, *McCormick*®
1	cup frozen chopped onion, *Ore-Ida*®
2	cans (10 ounces each) Mexican diced tomatoes, *Rotel*®
½	cup sliced green olives, *Early California*®
2	tablespoons capers, *Delallo*®
1	teaspoon crushed garlic, *Christopher Ranch*®
	Salt and pepper
¼	cup chopped fresh cilantro

1. In a large skillet, heat oil over medium-high heat. Add chicken and Mexican seasoning and sauté for 8 to 12 minutes, or until chicken is cooked through.

2. Add onion, tomatoes, olives, capers, and garlic. Stir to combine. Bring to a boil. Reduce heat and simmer for 5 minutes. Season to taste with salt and pepper. Stir in cilantro. Serve hot.

Cilantro-Garlic Potatoes

Start to Finish 10 minutes
Makes 4 servings

2	tablespoons extra virgin olive oil
⅓	cup peeled and diced red onion
¼	cup real bacon pieces, *Hormel*®
1	bag (16-ounce) precooked and diced red potatoes, *Reser's*®
1½	teaspoons crushed garlic, *Christopher Ranch*®
	Salt and pepper
¼	cup chopped fresh cilantro

1. In a large skillet, heat oil over medium-high heat. Add red onion and bacon pieces. Cook and stir until onion is soft, about 2 to 3 minutes.

2. Add potatoes and garlic. Cook 5 to 7 minutes, stirring occasionally. Season to taste with salt and pepper. Stir in cilantro and serve hot.

Pesto Chicken Panini

Start to Finish 10 minutes
Makes 4 servings

Serving Ideas:
Grill sandwich in
a grill pan or
panini press.

Tuscan Tomato Soup
with Basil (page 182)

¼   cup plus 2 tablespoons premade pesto, divided, *Delallo®*
¼   cup mayonnaise, *Best Foods®*
1   loaf (16-ounce) ciabatta bread, sliced in half horizontally
2   packages (6 ounces each) grilled chicken strips, *Oscar Mayer®*
1   cup baby arugula or spinach, rinsed and patted dry
2   tomatoes, sliced
15   fresh basil leaves
4   slices presliced mozzarella, *Tillamook®*

1. In a small bowl, stir together ¼ cup pesto and mayonnaise. Spread mixture on both sides of ciabatta. In a medium bowl, toss chicken strips with remaining 2 tablespoons pesto.

2. On bottom half of bread, place arugula, then pesto chicken mixture. Top with tomatoes, basil leaves, cheese, and top half of bread. Cut into 4 portions and serve.

Tuscan Tomato Soup with Basil

Start to Finish 10 minutes
Makes 4 servings

1	can (28-ounce) whole peeled tomatoes with basil, *Progresso*®
1	tablespoon extra virgin olive oil
1	cup frozen chopped onion, *Ore-Ida*®
1	teaspoon crushed garlic, *Christopher Ranch*®
1½	teaspoons Italian seasoning, *McCormick*®
1	cup white wine, Chardonnay
2	tablespoons chopped fresh basil leaves

1. Put tomatoes in a blender and puree.

2. In a medium pot, heat olive oil over medium-high heat. Add onion and garlic, and cook and stir for 1 to 2 minutes. Add pureed tomatoes, Italian seasoning, and wine. Bring to a boil. Reduce heat and simmer for 5 minutes. Serve garnished with chopped basil.

Bourbon
Chicken Sandwich

Start to Finish 10 minutes
Makes 4 servings

Serving Ideas:
Peach Tree Slaw
(page 186)

Kettle chips

½   cup peach preserves, *Smucker's*®
¼   cup chili sauce, *Heinz*®
2   tablespoons molasses, *Grandma's*®
¼   cup bourbon, *Jim Beam*®
2   packages (6 ounces each) grilled chicken strips, *Oscar Mayer*®
4   onion buns, split in half
4   leaves Bibb lettuce, rinsed and patted dry
2   tomatoes, sliced
     Red onion slices, peeled (optional)

1. In a medium skillet, over medium heat, melt peach preserves. Stir in chili sauce, molasses, and bourbon. Bring to a boil and add chicken strips. Stir and reduce heat. Simmer for 5 minutes. Meanwhile, on bottom half of buns, stack lettuce, sliced tomatoes, and red onion (optional).

2. Use tongs to remove chicken from sauce and divide among bottom halves of sandwich buns. Top with top halves of buns. Serve immediately with extra sauce on the side.

Peach Tree Slaw

Start to Finish 10 minutes
Makes 4 servings

1	container (6-ounce) peach yogurt, *Dannon®*
2	tablespoons mayonnaise, *Best Foods®*
2	tablespoons apple cider vinegar, *Heinz®*
6	cups 3-color coleslaw mix, *Fresh Express®*
2	cans (8 ounces each) diced peaches, drained, *Del Monte®*
½	cup chopped pecans, *Diamond®*

1. In a large bowl, whisk together yogurt, mayonnaise, and vinegar.

2. Add remaining ingredients and toss until thoroughly combined. Serve chilled or at room temperature.

BBQ Chicken Salad

Start to Finish 10 minutes
Makes 4 servings

Serving Ideas:
Chile and Cheddar
Corn Muffins
(see below)

10   cups (about 12 ounces) Italian lettuce mix, *Fresh Express*®
½   cup ranch salad dressing, *Hidden Valley*®
2   packages (6 ounces each) grilled chicken strips, *Oscar Mayer*®
⅓   cup BBQ sauce, *Bull's Eye*®
½   cup shredded cheddar cheese, *Kraft*®
1   can (11-ounce) mexicorn, *Green Giant*®
1   can (4-ounce) diced green chiles, *Ortega*®
¼   cup real crumbled bacon, *Hormel*®
1   cup french fried onions, *French's*®

1. In a large bowl, toss salad mix with ranch dressing and set aside. In a medium bowl, toss chicken strips with BBQ sauce and set aside.

2. Divide dressed salad among four chilled dinner plates. Top each with chicken strips. Compose salads with remaining ingredients. Serve immediately.

Chile and Cheddar Corn Muffins

Start to Finish 20 minutes
Makes 6 mini muffins

   Butter-flavored cooking spray
1   package (6.5-ounce) corn muffin mix, *Betty Crocker*®
⅓   cup milk
2   tablespoons butter, melted
1   egg
½   cup shredded cheddar cheese, *Kraft*®
1   can (4-ounce) diced green chiles, *Ortega*®
½   teaspoon ground black pepper

1. Preheat oven to 400 degrees F. Coat mini muffin pan with cooking spray. In a large bowl, combine all ingredients and stir until just moistened (batter will be lumpy). Spoon into prepared mini muffin cups.

2. Bake for 11 to 14 minutes, or until golden brown. Remove muffins from pan immediately and let cool on wire rack.

Turkey with Portobello Sauce

Start to Finish 20 minutes
Makes 4 servings

Turkey cutlets seared in olive oil can pass for veal, at a fraction of the cost. Woodsy portobello mushrooms and a farmer's market side, like Spinach and Tomatoes with Feta Cheese, complement without competing.

Serving Ideas:
Spinach and Tomatoes with Feta (page 193)

Rice pilaf, *Uncle Ben's® Ready Rice*

1¼   **pounds turkey cutlets, rinsed and patted dry**
1   **teaspoon garlic salt, *Lawry's®***
½   **teaspoon dried thyme, *McCormick®***
½   **teaspoon ground black pepper, *McCormick®***
2   **tablespoons extra virgin olive oil**
¼   **cup butter**
1   **package (8-ounce) presliced baby portobello mushrooms**
½   **cup Madeira wine, *Paul Masson®***
1   **cup low-sodium chicken broth, *Swanson®***
1   **packet (1.08-ounce) turkey gravy mix, *McCormick®***

1. Season both sides of cutlets with garlic salt, thyme, and pepper. In a large skillet, heat oil over medium-high heat. Add turkey cutlets and cook for 2 to 3 minutes per side, or until cooked through. Remove cutlets and set aside.

2. Melt butter in skillet. Add mushrooms and cook and stir for 5 minutes. Remove skillet from heat and carefully add Madeira wine. Return skillet to heat and deglaze by scraping brown bits from bottom of pan.

3. Add chicken broth and turkey gravy mix. Stir to combine and bring sauce to a boil. Return turkey cutlets and any accumulated juices to skillet. Reduce heat and simmer for 5 minutes, or until turkey is heated through. Serve turkey cutlets drizzled with portobello sauce.

Spinach and Tomatoes with Feta

Start to Finish 10 minutes
Makes 4 servings

2	tablespoons extra virgin olive oil
1	teaspoon crushed garlic, *Christopher Ranch®*
2	bags (12 ounces each) baby spinach, *Fresh Express®*
1	can (15-ounce) petite diced tomatoes, drained, *S&W®*
2	teaspoons lemon juice, *ReaLemon®*
1	package (4-ounce) crumbled feta cheese, *Athenos®*

1. In a large skillet, heat oil over medium-high heat. Add garlic and swirl around pan. Add spinach and sauté until almost wilted, using tongs to turn occasionally.

2. Add drained tomatoes and wilt spinach completely. Transfer to a serving bowl, stir in lemon juice, and top with crumbled feta cheese. Serve immediately.

Turkey Cutlets with Cranberry Chutney

Start to Finish 20 minutes
Makes 4 servings

Wait until Thanksgiving and you'll miss out on a well-kept secret: Turkey makes a delicious dinner year-round. Tart cranberry chutney unleashes the smoky flavor of the meat and merges well with nutty asparagus sauced with a lemony hollandaise.

FOR CRANBERRY CHUTNEY
- 1   cup whole cranberry sauce, *Ocean Spray*®
- 1   package (2.25-ounce) nut topping, *Diamond*®
- 1   teaspoon Chinese 5-spice powder, *McCormick*®
- 2   teaspoons orange zest
- 1   tablespoon raspberry vinegar, *Heinz*®

FOR TURKEY CUTLETS
- 1¼   pounds turkey cutlets, rinsed and patted dry
- ¾   teaspoon salt
- ½   teaspoon black pepper
- 2   teaspoons Chinese 5-spice powder, *McCormick*®
-   Flour, for dredging
- 2   tablespoons olive oil

1. For the cranberry chutney, stir together cranberry sauce, nut topping, 1 teaspoon 5-spice powder, orange zest, and vinegar in a medium bowl; set aside.

2. Season turkey cutlets on both sides with salt, pepper, and Chinese 5-spice powder. Dredge in flour, shaking to remove excess. Heat oil in a large skillet over medium-high heat. Sauté cutlets for 2 to 3 minutes per side, or until cooked through. Serve turkey cutlets topped with cranberry chutney.

Serving Ideas:
Roasted Asparagus with Lemony Hollandaise (page 197)

Mashed potatoes, *Country Crock Homestyle*®

Roasted Asparagus with Lemony Hollandaise

Start to Finish 20 minutes
Makes 4 servings

1   pound asparagus, cleaned and peeled (if necessary)
1   tablespoon extra virgin olive oil
     Lemon pepper, *Lawry's*®
1   can (6-ounce) Hollandaise sauce, *Aunt Penny's*®
2   teaspoons lemon juice, *ReaLemon*®
     Pinch cayenne pepper, *McCormick*®

1. Preheat oven to 400 degrees F. Line a heavy duty baking sheet with foil. Arrange asparagus on prepared baking sheet. Drizzle with olive oil and season to taste with lemon pepper. Toss to coat. Roast asparagus for 10 minutes, or until tender.

2. Meanwhile, transfer Hollandaise sauce to a microwave-safe bowl. Heat in microwave on HIGH for about 2 minutes, stirring every 30 seconds, until hot. Stir in lemon juice and cayenne. Serve asparagus hot with a dollop of Hollandaise sauce.

Olympic Hero

Start to Finish 10 minutes
Makes 4 sandwiches

The quintessentially Italian sub goes Greek, with lean turkey breast strips layered with oil-and-vinegar-seasoned romaine lettuce, tomatoes, kalamata olives, and feta cheese. Greek Garlic Fries dunked in gyro dressing scores a 10 as a side.

Serving Ideas:
Greek Garlic Fries
(page 201)

⅓ cup olive oil and vinegar dressing, *Newman's Own*®
1 tablespoon lemon juice, *ReaLemon*®
2 teaspoons Greek seasoning, *Spice Islands*®
1 package (10-ounce) precooked turkey breast strips, *Butterball*®
2 cups bagged, chopped romaine, *Fresh Express*®
2 tomatoes, diced
¼ cup peeled and slivered red onion
⅓ cup pitted Kalamata olives, *Peloponnese*®
1 package (4-ounce) crumbled feta cheese, *Athenos*®
4 hero sandwich rolls

1. In a large bowl, whisk together salad dressing, lemon juice, and Greek seasoning. Add all remaining ingredients to bowl and toss to combine with dressing.

2. Split hero rolls in half horizontally, but leave attached by one side; divide Greek salad among hero rolls.

Greek Garlic Fries

Start to Finish 10 minutes
Makes 4 servings

½   bag (26-ounce) frozen "fast food" fries, *Ore-Ida®*
2   tablespoons extra virgin olive oil
1½   teaspoons crushed garlic, *Christopher Ranch®*
1   teaspoon Greek seasoning, *Spice Islands®*
      Premade tzatziki or gyro dressing

1. Preheat broiler. On a heavy duty baking sheet, toss together fries, olive oil, garlic, and Greek seasoning. Arrange fries in a single layer.

2. Broil 6 inches from heat source for 5 to 8 minutes. Serve fries hot with tzatziki for dipping.

Tunisian Turkey Salad

Start to Finish 10 minutes
Makes 4 servings

1	package (10-ounce) precooked turkey strips, *Butterball*®
1	can (15-ounce) low-sodium garbanzo beans, drained, *S&W*®
¼	cup dried cranberries, *Ocean Spray*®
2	scallions, thinly sliced
2	tablespoons chopped fresh flat leaf parsley
½	cup poppy seed dressing, *Brianna's*®
2	tablespoons honey, *Sue Bee*®
¼	teaspoon ground cinnamon, *McCormick*®
¼	teaspoon cayenne pepper, *McCormick*®
10	cups bagged chopped romaine, *Fresh Express*®
2	tomatoes, cut into wedges
½	cucumber, thinly sliced
¼	chopped pistachios, *Diamond*® (optional)

Serving Ideas:
Curried Apple Squash Soup (page 205)

Toasted flatbread

1. In a large bowl, combine turkey, garbanzo beans, cranberries, scallions, and parsley. In a small bowl, stir together poppy seed dressing, honey, cinnamon, and cayenne pepper. Pour over turkey mixture and toss to combine.

2. Divide chopped romaine among 4 chilled dinner plates. Top with turkey mixture. Compose salads with tomato wedges and cucumbers. Serve immediately, garnished with pistachios (optional).

Curried Apple Squash Soup

Start to Finish 10 minutes
Makes 4 servings

2   **boxes (18.3 ounces each) butternut squash soup,**
      ***Campbell's Select*®**
1   **cup cinnamon apple sauce, *Mott's*®**
2   **tablespoons ketchup, *Heinz*®**
2   **teaspoons curry powder, *McCormick*®**
1   **teaspoon pumpkin pie spice, *McCormick*®**
      Plain yogurt or sour cream (optional)

1. In a medium saucepan, over medium-high heat, combine all ingredients, except yogurt. Bring to boil.

2. Reduce heat and simmer for 5 minutes. Serve hot with a drizzle of plain yogurt or sour cream (optional).

Treats and Desserts

Dessert is a delicious dilemma. Do we watch every bite or just toss caution—and calories—to the wind and say, "It's worth it!" The older I get, the more health-conscious I become. And while I'll give up many things, I always save room for dessert. Whether it's good-for-you fruit or dare-to-be-decadent cake, dessert is something to look forward to, a chance to savor joy wherever it comes, even if it's on a plate. Pink Strawberry or Apple Cinnamon Popcorn gives a salty snack a sugary spin. A Jelly Bean Cocktail gets any evening off to a lively start, while Tiramisu a l'Orange makes an elegant finisher. And if it's pure indulgence you're after, Chocolate Caramel-Corn Candy Cubes are a triple treat, after a special dinner, an everyday dinner, or even just for dinner.

The Recipes

Almond Joy Layer Cake	209
Blueberry Lemon Cake	210
Pecan Cinnamon Angel Food Cake	213
No-Bake Birthday Cake	214
Tiramisu a l'Orange	217
Tropical Trifle	218
Banana Toffee Pie	221
Creamy Pudding Four Ways	222
Brandied Cherry Crepes	225
Chocolate Caramel-Corn	
Candy Cubes	226
Pink Strawberry Popcorn	229
Apple Cinnamon Popcorn	229
Cocktails	
Jelly Bean Cocktail	230
Peach Blossom Cocktail	230
Strawberry Creamsicle Martini	233
Sandra's Express-O Cocktail	233

Almond Joy Layer Cake

Start to Finish 20 minutes
Makes 8 servings

If I could have my pick of candy bars, I'd choose Almond Joy®, so reinventing that irresistible blend of sweet coconut, smoky almonds, and creamy milk chocolate as a four-layer cake was a labor of love. Chopped peanuts add a satisfying crunch.

2 (8-inch) round, store-bought chocolate cake layers
2 cans (16 ounces each) chocolate frosting, divided, *Betty Crocker Rich & Creamy®*
2 teaspoons almond extract, divided, *McCormick®*
1 cup flake coconut, *Baker's®*
1 package (2-ounce) nut topping, *Planters®*

1. Cut each cake layer in half horizontally to make a total of four layers. In a small bowl, stir together 1 container of chocolate frosting, 1 teaspoon of the almond extract, the coconut, and nut topping.

2. To assemble cake: Spread chocolate coconut filling mixture evenly on 3 of the layers. Place the fourth layer on top. Stir remaining 1 teaspoon almond extract into remaining container of chocolate frosting and frost outside of cake.

Blueberry Lemon Cake

Start to Finish 20 minutes
Makes 10 servings

2   (8-inch) round, store-bought yellow or white cake layers
⅓   cup frozen lemonade concentrate, thawed, *Minute Maid*®
2   teaspoons lemon extract, divided, *McCormick*®
2   cans (12 ounces each) cream cheese-flavored frosting,
      Betty Crocker®
      Fresh mint sprigs
      Fresh blueberries
      Thin lemon slices

1. Use a knife to slice cake layers in half horizontally, to make a total of 4 layers. Use a pastry brush to brush each layer with lemonade concentrate; set aside. Stir 1 teaspoon of lemon extract into each can of frosting; set aside.

2. To assemble cake: Use 1½ cans of the frosting to frost and stack the cake layers on top of each other. Use remaining frosting to frost the top of the cake. Decorate cake with mint leaves, blueberries, and lemon slices.

Pecan Cinnamon Angel Food Cake

Start to Finish 20 minutes
Makes 8 servings

1   teaspoon cinnamon extract, *McCormick*®
1   container (16-ounce) whipped topping, divided, *Cool Whip*®
1   (10-inch) store-bought angel food cake
¼   cup cream cheese, *Philadelphia*®
2   tablespoons light brown sugar, *C&H*®
½   cup chopped pecans, *Diamond*®
1   teaspoon ground cinnamon, *McCormick*®
    Chopped pecans (optional)

1. Stir cinnamon extract into whipped topping container; set aside. Carefully slice off 1-inch top layer from angel food cake; set aside. Cut down into cake and gently remove core of cake, leaving a 1-inch-thick border from bottom and around sides. Crumble cored cake into small pieces.

2. In a medium bowl, stir together cake pieces, cream cheese, brown sugar, pecans, and cinnamon. Gently fold in 1 cup whipped topping. Fill center of cake with mixture. Place cake top back on. Frost cake with remaining whipped topping. Garnish with chopped pecans (optional).

No-Bake Birthday Cake

Start to Finish 20 minutes
Makes 25 servings

Towers of store-bought cake, cupcakes, and cookies, decorated with swirls of colored frosting, make this no-bake cake a never-ending adventure. Personalize it with a theme—sports, flowers, or a day at the beach—to make any birthday super-special.

1   bakery-bought half-sheet cake, frosted white and bordered in color of your choice
1   bakery-bought 8-inch layer cake, frosted white and bordered in color of your choice
8   bakery-bought cupcakes with white frosting
8   theme-decorated cookies (i.e., birthday packages, sports, beach, sun and moon, etc.)
     Writing frosting, *CakeMate*®
     Fancy birthday candles

1. Cut dowels to the height of the sheet cake. Sink dowels around the center of the sheet cake to support the layer cake. Place the 8-inch layer cake in the center of sheet cake (on top of the dowels). Place 4 of the cupcakes on top of the layer cake; add 1 cookie in the center of the 4 cupcakes. Place the 4 remaining cupcakes on the corners of the sheet cake.

2. Decorate with cookies around cakes, pressing gently into frosting and/or inserting into the cupcakes. Use writing frosting for birthday wishes and place appropriate number of candles.

Tiramisu à l'Orange

Start to Finish 20 minutes
Makes 4 servings

1	teaspoon (rounded) instant espresso powder, *Medaglia D'Oro®*
⅓	cup *Grand Marnier®*
16	to 24 ladyfinger cookies
1	box (1-ounce) sugar-free cheesecake-flavored instant pudding mix, *Jell-O®*
1¾	cups milk
1	teaspoon orange extract, *McCormick®*
	Cocoa powder, for dusting

1. In a shallow bowl, stir espresso powder into ⅓ cup warm water until dissolved. Stir in Grand Marnier®. Dip ladyfingers into espresso mixture and line the sides of 4 parfait or wine glasses; set aside.

2. In a large bowl, whisk together pudding mix, milk, and orange extract for 2 minutes. Divide pudding mixture among the ladyfinger-lined glasses. Let sit for 5 minutes. Dust tops with cocoa powder and serve.

Tropical Trifle

Start to Finish 20 minutes
Makes 4 servings

16	soft macaroon cookies, *Archway*®
⅓	cup pineapple rum, *Malibu*®
1	box (1.4-ounce) instant vanilla pudding mix, *Jell-O*®
2	cups cold milk
1	teaspoon rum extract, *McCormick*®
2	containers (8 ounces each) refrigerated tropical fruit medley, drained, *Del Monte Fruit Naturals*®
	Finely chopped macadamia nuts (optional)
	Fresh mint sprigs (optional)

1. Break up macaroons and place in a shallow bowl. Pour rum over the top and let macaroons soak in the rum for 2 to 3 minutes. Drain and set aside.

2. Meanwhile, in a medium bowl whisk together the pudding mix, cold milk, and rum extract. Whisk for 2 minutes until the pudding thickens; set aside.

3. In 4 separate wine glasses, layer the macaroons, drained fruit, and pudding. Garnish with chopped nuts (optional) and fresh mint sprigs (optional).

Banana Toffee Pie

Start to Finish 20 minutes
Makes 8 servings

This silky cream pie duplicates the down-home appeal of banana pudding and gives it an uptown makeover at the same time. Gloriously gooey caramel sets it apart, while crumbled Heath® bars sprinkled on the top and bottom add a final flourish.

¾   cup toffee bits, divided, *Heath*®
1   (9-inch) graham cracker crumb pie crust, *Keebler*®
1   box (5.1-ounce) vanilla-flavored instant pudding mix, *Jell-O*®
2¼ cups milk
¼   cup caramel topping, *Hershey's*®
     Bananas, peeled and sliced
1   container (8-ounce) whipped topping, *Cool Whip*®

1. Sprinkle ½ cup of the toffee bits in an even layer on the bottom of crust. Set aside. In a large bowl, whisk together pudding mix, milk, and caramel topping for 2 minutes. Fill pie crust with pudding mixture.

2. Arrange sliced bananas on top of pudding. Top with whipped topping and sprinkle with the remaining ¼ cup toffee bits. Slice and serve immediately.

Creamy Pudding Four Ways

Start to Finish 20 minutes
Makes 6 servings

VARIATIONS
Substitute chocolate chips with any of the following:

peanut butter chips
white chocolate chips
butterscotch chips

⅓   **cup granulated sugar**
3   **tablespoons cornstarch**
2   **cups milk**
1   **bag (11-ounce) milk chocolate chips, *Hershey's*®**
1   **teaspoon vanilla extract, *McCormick*®**

1. In a medium heavy-bottom saucepan, over medium heat, stir together sugar and cornstarch. Gradually stir in milk. Heat mixture, stirring constantly, until it begins to boil and thicken, about 8 to 10 minutes.

2. Reduce heat to medium-low and stir in chocolate chips. Continue stirring until smooth and chocolate chips have melted. Pour into serving cups and let stand 5 minutes. Serve warm or chilled.

Brandied Cherry Crepes

Start to Finish 20 minutes
Makes 6 servings

1   can (21-ounce) cherry pie filling, *Comstock More Fruit*®
¼   cup kirsch (cherry brandy)
4   tablespoons butter, cold
6   store-bought crepes, *Frieda's*®
      Chocolate syrup, *Hershey's*®
      Fresh mint sprigs (optional)

1. In a medium saucepan, combine pie filling and brandy. Bring to a boil over medium heat. Reduce to simmer Cut cold butter into 1 tablespoon pats and stir in one at a time until melted. Remove from heat.

2. Divide cherries among the 6 crepes and roll or fold crepes. Top with a little chocolate syrup and garnish with a sprig of mint (optional).

Chocolate Caramel Corn Candy Cubes

Start to Finish 20 minutes
Makes 4 servings

These bonbons are delicious on so many levels, from their *Kit Kat®* crust to their *Cracker Jack®* center, drizzled with layer upon layer of chocolate and caramel, chilled to a crunchy candy shell. Kids can make them in the microwave… as long as they share!

4	candy bars, (1.5 ounces each), *Kit Kat®*
3	boxes (1.0 ounces each) caramel corn with peanuts, *Cracker Jack®*
15	individually wrapped caramels, *Kraft®*
1¼	teaspoons butter
½	cup white chocolate chips, *Nestle®*
½	cup milk chocolate chips, *Nestle®*
3	teaspoons shortening, divided, *Crisco®*

1. Unwrap candy bars and place face down on waxed or parchment paper; set aside. Pour caramel corn in a medium bowl; set aside.

2. In one microwave-safe bowl, combine caramels with butter. In another bowl, combine white chocolate with 1½ teaspoons shortening. In a third bowl, combine chocolate chips with remaining shortening.

3. Heat one bowl at a time in microwave on HIGH heat for about 2 minutes, stirring every 30 seconds until contents are completely melted. Drizzle half of melted caramel over each candy bar. Divide and mound caramel corn on top of each bar. Drizzle the melted white chocolate, remaining melted caramel, and melted milk chocolate over caramel corn. Place in refrigerator for 5 minutes to set.

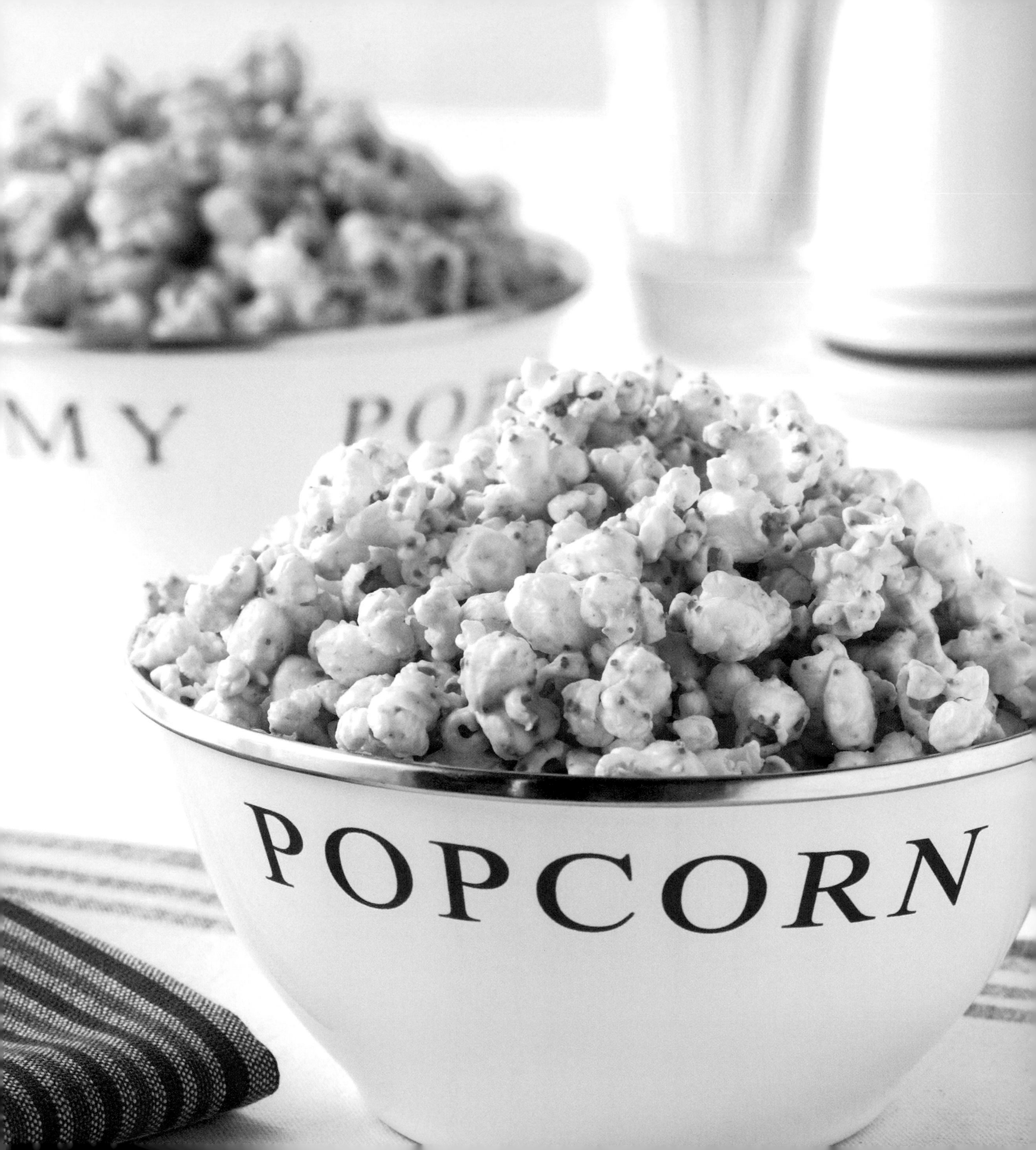
POPCORN

Pink Strawberry Popcorn

Start to Finish 10 minutes
Makes 14 cups

1	tablespoon shortening, *Crisco®*
1	packet (0.14-ounce) strawberry-flavored drink mix, *Kool-Aid®*
1	bag (12-ounce) white chocolate chips, *Nestle®*
2	drops red food coloring, gel or paste (optional)
2	bags (3 ounces each) microwave popcorn, popped, *Orville® Redenbacher's Tender White®*
3	tablespoons pink sanding sugar

1. In a microwave-safe bowl, combine shortening and drink mix. Melt in microwave on HIGH heat for 1 minute. Remove and stir. Add white chocolate chips. Return to microwave and melt chips on LOW heat for 2 minutes, stirring every 30 seconds. (If using food coloring, stir into melted chocolate at this point.)

2. In a large bowl, slowly pour melted white chocolate mixture over popped popcorn, tossing with wooden spoon. Sprinkle sanding sugar over the top and toss to coat.

Tip: Gel or paste food coloring is available at cake decorating stores. DO NOT USE LIQUID food coloring as it will cause chocolate to seize.

Apple Cinnamon Popcorn

Start to Finish 10 minutes
Makes 14 cups

2	bags (3 ounces each) microwave popcorn, popped, *Orville Redenbacher Tender White®*
1½	cups dried sliced apples, finely chopped, *Mariani®*
¼	cup butter
3	tablespoons water
¾	cup light brown sugar, *C&H®*
2	teaspoons ground cinnamon, *McCormick®*

1. In a large bowl, combine popped popcorn and dried apples; set aside. In a medium saucepan, over medium-high heat, melt butter. Add water, brown sugar, and cinnamon. Bring to boil and cook for 1 minute.

2. Carefully pour brown sugar mixture over popcorn-apple mixture, tossing with wooden spoon.

Jelly Bean Cocktail

Start to Finish 5 minutes
Makes 1 cocktail

1   shot grape juice
1   shot raspberry liquer, *Chambord*®
1   shot vanilla vodka, *Stoli Vanil*®
     Lemon twist (optional)

1. Combine all ingredients in a martini shaker filled with ice.

2. Shake vigorously. Strain into a martini glass and garnish with a twist of lemon (optional).

Peach Blossom Cocktail

Start to Finish 5 minutes
Makes 1 cocktail

1   shot peach vodka, *Absolut Peach*®
2   shots peach nectar, *Kern's*®
½   shot peach schnapps, *DeKuyper*®
     Splash lime juice, *ReaLime*®
     Edible flowers (optional)

1. Combine all ingredients in a martini shaker filled with ice. Shake vigorously.

2. Strain into a martini glass. Garnish with an edible flower (optional).

Strawberry
Creamsicle Martini

Start to Finish 5 minutes
Makes 1 cocktail

1	shot vanilla vodka, *Stoli Vanil*®
½	shot strawberry nectar, *Kern's*®
½	shot strawberry liqueur, *Bols*®
1	shot half-and-half
	Fresh strawberry (optional)

1. Combine all ingredients in a martini shaker filled with ice. Shake vigorously.

2. Strain into a chilled martini glass. Garnish with a strawberry (optional).

Sandra's
Express-O Cocktail

Start to Finish 5 minutes
Makes 1 cocktail

½	teaspoon instant espresso powder, *Medaglia D'Oro*®
¼	cup warm water
1	shot vanilla vodka, *Stoli Vanil*®
½	shot *Bailey's Irish Cream*®

1. Stir espresso powder into warm water until dissolved. Pour espresso and remaining ingredients into a martini shaker filled with ice. Shake vigorously.

2. Strain into a rocks glass filled with ice.

Index

A

Almond Brown Butter, Broccoli with, 143
Almond Joy Layer Cake, 209
Appetizers. *See Starters and snacks*
Apples
    Apple Cinnamon Popcorn, 229
    Curried Apple Squash Soup, 205
Artichokes
    Artichoke Focaccini, 26
    Bow Ties with Artichoke Pesto, 54
    Fried Cheese Ravioli with Tomato Pepper Relish and Artichoke Caper Dip, 21
    Lemon Artichokes and Capers, 155
    Warm Spinach Salad with Eggs and Bacon, 42
Arugula Salad with Pears and Gorgonzola, 50
Asparagus
    Bulgur with Asparagus and Feta, 110
    Prosciutto-Tied Asparagus, 25
    Roasted Asparagus with Lemony Hollandaise, 197
    Roasted Asparagus with Portobello Mushrooms, 62
Avocados
    Chilled Avocado Soup, 147
    Shrimp with Avocado in Tequila Cream Sauce, 135

B

Bacon
    Blue Cheese and Bacon Mashed Potatoes, 70
    Mixed Greens Salad with Fingerlings and Bacon, 116
    Trout BLT, 131
    Warm Spinach Salad with Eggs and Bacon, 42
Balsamic Melon Salad, 101
Balsamic Roasted Tomatoes, 57
Banana Toffee Pie, 221
BBQ Chicken Salad, 189
Beans. *See also Green beans*
    Black Bean and Spinach Couscous, 169
    Black Bean Salad, 78
    Green Chile Pintos, 98
    Tunisian Turkey Salad, 202
Beef
    Filet Mignon with Red Wine Mushrooms, 69
    Rib-Eye Steaks with Cognac-Peppercorn Sauce, 73
    Roast Beef and Blue Cheese Tea Sandwiches, 30
    Steak House Salad with Horseradish Dressing, 74
    Western Meatloaf Sandwich, 78
Beer Battered Onion Rings, 77
Black Bean and Spinach Couscous, 169
Black Bean Salad, 78
Blueberry Lemon Cake, 210

Blue Cheese and Bacon Mashed Potatoes, 70
Bourbon Chicken Sandwich, 185
Bourbon Creamed Corn, 94
Bow Ties with Artichoke Pesto, 54
Brandied Cherry Crepes, 225
Breads
    Chile and Cheddar Corn Muffins, 189
    Mozzarella Garlic Bread, 37
    Prosciutto-Wrapped Breadsticks, 46
Broccoli
    Broccoli with Almond Brown Butter, 143
    Creamy Cheesy Potatoes and Broccoli, 73
    Fresh Broccoli Salad, 46
    Minted Broccoli Slaw, 105
Bulgur with Asparagus and Feta, 110

C

Cabbage
    Jicama Slaw, 135
    Peach Tree Slaw, 186
    Siam Peanut Slaw, 123
Cakes
    Almond Joy Layer Cake, 209
    Blueberry Lemon Cake, 210
    No-Bake Birthday Cake, 214
    Pecan Cinnamon Angel Food Cake, 213
Captain's Club with Shrimp and Chipotle Mayonnaise, 144
Caramel-Corn Candy Cubes, Chocolate, 226
Carnitas Tacos, 97
Carrots and Snap Peas, Glazed, with Golden Raisins, 106
Cheese
    Arugula Salad with Pears and Gorgonzola, 50
    Blue Cheese and Bacon Mashed Potatoes, 70
    Bulgur with Asparagus and Feta, 110
    Chile and Cheddar Corn Muffins, 189
    Chili Cheese Slices, 26
    Creamy Cheesy Potatoes and Broccoli, 73
    Crostini with Shrimp and Boursin Cheese, 25
    Fettucini with Parmesan Sauce, 90
    French Brie and Ham Baguette Tea Sandwiches, 30
    Greek Layered Dip with Pita Chips, 18
    Haricots Verts with Shaved Parmesan, 38
    Mozzarella Garlic Bread, 37
    Olympic Hero, 198
    Roast Beef and Blue Cheese Tea Sandwiches, 30
    Shrimp and Cheesy Grits, 136
    Soft Goat Cheese Polenta, 86
    Spinach and Tomatoes with Feta, 193
    Venetian Ham Panini, 101
    Warm Orzo Salad with Peas, Mint, and Feta, 162
Cherry Crepes, Brandied, 225
Chicken
    BBQ Chicken Salad, 189
    Bourbon Chicken Sandwich, 185
    Chicken and Mushrooms in Creamy Tarragon Sauce, 174
    Chicken Caesar Focaccia Sandwiches with Rosemary Skewers, 29

Chicken Pasta Milanese, 34
    Chicken Vera Cruz, 177
    Chicken with Lemon-Thyme Brown Butter, 161
    Chicken with Peach and Melon Salsa, 166
    Creamy Chicken Mini Pitas, 29
    Orange-Walnut Pesto Chicken, 165
    Pesto Chicken Panini, 181
    Wasabi Chicken, 170
Chiles
    Chile and Cheddar Corn Muffins, 189
    Fiesta Tomato Soup, 156
    Green Chile Pintos, 98
Chili Cheese Slices, 26
Chilled Avocado Soup, 147
Chocolate
    Almond Joy Layer Cake, 209
    Chocolate Caramel-Corn Candy Cubes, 226
    Creamy Pudding Four Ways, 222
Chowder, Scallop and Mushroom, 148
Cilantro-Garlic Potatoes, 178
Clams
    Sicilian Steamers, 152
Cocktails
    Jelly Bean Cocktail, 230
    Peach Blossom Cocktail, 230
    premade mixes for, 15
    Sandra's Express-O Cocktail, 233
    Strawberry Creamsicle Martini, 233
Coconut
    Almond Joy Layer Cake, 209
Corn
    BBQ Chicken Salad, 189
    Bourbon Creamed Corn, 94
    Fiesta Tomato Soup, 156
Corn Muffins, Chile and Cheddar, 189
Couscous
    Black Bean and Spinach Couscous, 169
    Mandarin Couscous, 119
Crab Cake Fritters, 22
Crab Parfait, 156
Cranberry Chutney, Turkey Cutlets with, 194
Creamy Cheesy Potatoes and Broccoli, 73
Creamy Chicken Mini Pitas, 29
Creamy Pudding Four Ways, 222
Creamy Red Potato Salad with Green Olives and Capers, 132
Crepes, Brandied Cherry, 225
Crostini with Shrimp and Boursin Cheese, 25
Curried Apple Squash Soup, 205

D

Desserts
    Almond Joy Layer Cake, 209
    Apple Cinnamon Popcorn, 229
    Banana Toffee Pie, 221
    Blueberry Lemon Cake, 210
    Brandied Cherry Crepes, 225
    Chocolate Caramel-Corn Candy Cubes, 226
    Creamy Pudding Four Ways, 222
    No-Bake Birthday Cake, 214
    Pecan Cinnamon Angel Food Cake, 213
    Pink Strawberry Popcorn, 229
    Tiramisù à l'Orange, 217
    Tropical Trifle, 218

Dips
Fried Cheese Ravioli with Tomato Pepper Relish and Artichoke Caper Dip, 21
Greek Layered Dip with Pita Chips, 18

E
Eggs and Bacon, Warm Spinach Salad with, 42
Entrées (meat)
Carnitas Tacos, 97
Filet Mignon with Red Wine Mushrooms, 69
Lamb and Olive Skewers, 109
Lamb Chops with Garlic Yogurt Sauce, 106
Lamb Chops with Mango Chutney, 102
Pork Loin Chops with Peach BBQ Sauce, 93
Pork Medallions with Creamy Pesto Sauce, 85
Pork Piccata with Wilted Spinach, 89
Pork Tenderloin with Apple-Jack Sauce, 81
Rib-Eye Steaks with Cognac-Peppercorn Sauce, 73
Steak House Salad with Horseradish Dressing, 74
Venetian Ham Panini, 101
Western Meatloaf Sandwich, 78
Entrées (pasta)
Angel Hair with Salmon in Lemon Cream Sauce, 49
Bow Ties with Artichoke Pesto, 54
Chicken Pasta Milanese, 34
Fettucini with Lobster Sauce, 38
Linguine with Vegetable Alfredo, 41
Linguine with Zucchini Caponata, 45
Orecchiette with Sweet Red Pepper Sauce, 58
Penne Niçoise, 50
Penne Puttanesca, 53
Ravioli Balsamico, 62
Ravioli with Marsala-Caper Sauce, 65
Entrées (poultry)
BBQ Chicken Salad, 189
Bourbon Chicken Sandwich, 185
Chicken and Mushrooms in Creamy Tarragon Sauce, 174
Chicken Vera Cruz, 177
Chicken with Lemon-Thyme Brown Butter, 161
Chicken with Peach and Melon Salsa, 166
Olympic Hero, 198
Orange-Walnut Pesto Chicken, 165
Pesto Chicken Panini, 181
Tunisian Turkey Salad, 202
Turkey Cutlets with Cranberry Chutney, 194
Turkey with Portobello Sauce, 190
Wasabi Chicken, 170
Entrées (seafood)
Captain's Club with Shrimp and Chipotle Mayonnaise, 144
Crab Parfait, 156
Halibut with Champagne Mushroom Sauce, 127
Orange Balsamic Glazed Salmon, 119
Salmon with Chili-Lime Hollandaise, 115
Scallop and Mushroom Chowder, 148
Shrimp and Cheesy Grits, 136

Shrimp with Avocado in Tequila Cream Sauce, 135
Sicilian Steamers, 152
Swordfish with Ginger-Garlic Sauce, 120
Tarragon Garlic Shrimp Skewers, 140
Trout BLT, 131
Wine Poached Tilapia with Herb Sauce, 124

F
Fettucini with Lobster Sauce, 38
Fettucini with Parmesan Sauce, 90
Fiesta Tomato Soup, 156
Filet Mignon with Red Wine Mushrooms, 69
Fish. *See also Shellfish*
Angel Hair with Salmon in Lemon Cream Sauce, 49
Halibut with Champagne Mushroom Sauce, 127
Orange Balsamic Glazed Salmon, 119
Penne Niçoise, 50
Salmon with Chili-Lime Hollandaise, 115
Swordfish with Ginger-Garlic Sauce, 120
Trout BLT, 131
Wine Poached Tilapia with Herb Sauce, 124
Four Pea Stir-Fry, 173
French Brie and Ham Baguette Tea Sandwiches, 30
Fresh Broccoli Salad, 46
Fried Cheese Ravioli with Tomato Pepper Relish and Artichoke Caper Dip, 21
Fritters, Crab Cake, 22
Fruit. *See also specific fruits*
Tropical Trifle, 218

G
Garlic
Garlicky Sautéed Green Beans and Peas, 49
Greek Garlic Fries, 201
Mozzarella Garlic Bread, 37
Sautéed Zucchini with Garlic and Herbs, 65
Ginger-Garlic Sauce, Swordfish with, 120
Glazed Carrots and Snap Peas with Golden Raisins, 106
Greek Garlic Fries, 201
Greek Layered Dip with Pita Chips, 18
Green beans
Garlicky Sautéed Green Beans and Peas, 49
Green Beans with Brown Butter and Pine Nuts, 124
Haricots Verts with Shaved Parmesan, 38
Penne Niçoise, 50
Green Chile Pintos, 98
Greens. *See also Spinach*
Arugula Salad with Pears and Gorgonzola, 50
BBQ Chicken Salad, 189
Mixed Greens Salad with Fingerlings and Bacon, 116
Mixed Greens with Mandarin Oranges and Walnuts, 37
Steak House Salad with Horseradish Dressing, 74
Tunisian Turkey Salad, 202
Grits, Cheesy, and Shrimp, 136

H
Halibut with Champagne Mushroom Sauce, 127
Ham
French Brie and Ham Baguette Tea Sandwiches, 30
Prosciutto-Tied Asparagus, 25
Prosciutto-Wrapped Breadsticks, 46
Venetian Ham Panini, 101
Haricots Verts with Shaved Parmesan, 38
Herbed Rice Pilaf, 128

J
Jelly Bean Cocktail, 230
Jicama Slaw, 135

L
Lamb
Greek Layered Dip with Pita Chips, 18
Lamb and Olive Skewers, 109
Lamb Chops with Garlic Yogurt Sauce, 106
Lamb Chops with Mango Chutney, 102
Lemon
Blueberry Lemon Cake, 210
Lemon Artichokes and Capers, 155
Linguine with Vegetable Alfredo, 41
Linguine with Zucchini Caponata, 45
Lobster Sauce, Fettucini with, 38

M
Mandarin Couscous, 119
Mangos
Lamb Chops with Mango Chutney, 102
Spinach Salad with Mangos and Mandarins, 151
Maple Sweet Potatoes, 82
Meat. *See Beef; Lamb; Pork*
Meatloaf Sandwich, Western, 78
Melon
Balsamic Melon Salad, 101
Chicken with Peach and Melon Salsa, 166
Minted Broccoli Slaw, 105
Mixed Greens Salad with Fingerlings and Bacon, 116
Mixed Greens with Mandarin Oranges and Walnuts, 37
Mozzarella Garlic Bread, 37
Muffins, Chile and Cheddar Corn, 189
Mushrooms
Chicken and Mushrooms in Creamy Tarragon Sauce, 174
Filet Mignon with Red Wine Mushrooms, 69
Halibut with Champagne Mushroom Sauce, 127
Roasted Asparagus with Portobello Mushrooms, 62
Scallop and Mushroom Chowder, 148
Turkey with Portobello Sauce, 190

N
No-Bake Birthday Cake, 214
Nuts. *See also Walnuts*
Almond Joy Layer Cake, 209

Index

Broccoli with Almond Brown Butter, 143
Green Beans with Brown Butter and Pine Nuts, 124
Nutty Herbed Rice, 174
Pecan Cinnamon Angel Food Cake, 213
Siam Peanut Slaw, 123

O
Olives
Chicken Vera Cruz, 177
Creamy Red Potato Salad with Green Olives and Capers, 132
Lamb and Olive Skewers, 109
Olympic Hero, 198
Olympic Hero, 198
Onion Rings, Beer Battered, 77
Oranges
Jicama Slaw, 135
Mandarin Couscous, 119
Mixed Greens with Mandarin Oranges and Walnuts, 37
Orange Balsamic Glazed Salmon, 119
Orange-Walnut Pesto Chicken, 165
Spinach Salad with Mangos and Mandarins, 151
Orecchiette with Sweet Red Pepper Sauce, 58
Orzo Salad, Warm, with Peas, Mint, and Feta, 162

P
Pasta
Angel Hair with Salmon in Lemon Cream Sauce, 49
Black Bean and Spinach Couscous, 169
Bow Ties with Artichoke Pesto, 54
Chicken Pasta Milanese, 34
Fettucini with Lobster Sauce, 38
Fettucini with Parmesan Sauce, 90
Fried Cheese Ravioli with Tomato Pepper Relish and Artichoke Caper Dip, 21
Linguine with Vegetable Alfredo, 41
Linguine with Zucchini Caponata, 45
Mandarin Couscous, 119
Orecchiette with Sweet Red Pepper Sauce, 58
Penne Niçoise, 50
Penne Puttanesca, 53
Ravioli Balsamico, 62
Ravioli with Marsala-Caper Sauce, 65
Sicilian Steamers, 152
Warm Orzo Salad with Peas, Mint, and Feta, 162
Peach Blossom Cocktail, 230
Peaches
Chicken with Peach and Melon Salsa, 166
Peach Tree Slaw, 186
Pork Loin Chops with Peach BBQ Sauce, 93
Peanut Slaw, Siam, 123
Pears and Gorgonzola, Arugula Salad with, 50
Peas
Four Pea Stir-Fry, 173

Garlicky Sautéed Green Beans and Peas, 49
Glazed Carrots and Snap Peas with Golden Raisins, 106
Linguine with Vegetable Alfredo, 41
Warm Orzo Salad with Peas, Mint, and Feta, 162
Pecan Cinnamon Angel Food Cake, 213
Penne Niçoise, 50
Penne Puttanesca, 53
Peppers. *See also Chiles*
Fried Cheese Ravioli with Tomato Pepper Relish and Artichoke Caper Dip, 21
Linguine with Vegetable Alfredo, 41
Orecchiette with Sweet Red Pepper Sauce, 58
Pesto Chicken, Orange-Walnut, 165
Pesto Chicken Panini, 181
Pesto Sauce, Creamy, Pork Medallions with, 85
Pie, Banana Toffee, 221
Pink Strawberry Popcorn, 229
Pita Chips, Greek Layered Dip with, 18
Pitas, Mini, Creamy Chicken, 29
Polenta, Soft Goat Cheese, 86
Popcorn
Apple Cinnamon Popcorn, 229
Chocolate Caramel-Corn Candy Cubes, 226
Pink Strawberry Popcorn, 229
Pork. *See also Bacon; Ham*
Carnitas Tacos, 97
Pork Loin Chops with Peach BBQ Sauce, 93
Pork Medallions with Creamy Pesto Sauce, 85
Pork Piccata with Wilted Spinach, 89
Pork Tenderloin with Apple-Jack Sauce, 81
Potatoes
Blue Cheese and Bacon Mashed Potatoes, 70
Cilantro-Garlic Potatoes, 178
Creamy Cheesy Potatoes and Broccoli, 73
Creamy Red Potato Salad with Green Olives and Capers, 132
Greek Garlic Fries, 201
Mixed Greens Salad with Fingerlings and Bacon, 116
Penne Niçoise, 50
Ranch Mashed Potatoes, 165
Poultry. *See Chicken; Turkey*
Prosciutto-Tied Asparagus, 25
Prosciutto-Wrapped Breadsticks, 46
Puddings
Creamy Pudding Four Ways, 222
Tiramisù à l'Orange, 217
Tropical Trifle, 218

R
Ranch Mashed Potatoes, 165
Ravioli
Fried Cheese Ravioli with Tomato Pepper Relish and Artichoke Caper Dip, 21
Ravioli Balsamico, 62
Ravioli with Marsala-Caper Sauce, 65
Rib-Eye Steaks with Cognac-Peppercorn Sauce, 73

Rice, Nutty Herbed, 174
Rice Pilaf, Herbed, 128
Roast Beef and Blue Cheese Tea Sandwiches, 30
Roasted Asparagus with Lemony Hollandaise, 197
Roasted Asparagus with Portobello Mushrooms, 62

S
Salad Bar Stir-Fry, 61
Salads
Arugula Salad with Pears and Gorgonzola, 50
Balsamic Melon Salad, 101
BBQ Chicken Salad, 189
Black Bean Salad, 78
Creamy Red Potato Salad with Green Olives and Capers, 132
Fresh Broccoli Salad, 46
Jicama Slaw, 135
Minted Broccoli Slaw, 105
Mixed Greens Salad with Fingerlings and Bacon, 116
Mixed Greens with Mandarin Oranges and Walnuts, 37
Peach Tree Slaw, 186
Siam Peanut Slaw, 123
Spinach Salad with Mangos and Mandarins, 151
Steak House Salad with Horseradish Dressing, 74
Tunisian Turkey Salad, 202
Warm Orzo Salad with Peas, Mint, and Feta, 162
Warm Spinach Salad with Eggs and Bacon, 42
Salmon
Angel Hair with Salmon in Lemon Cream Sauce, 49
Orange Balsamic Glazed Salmon, 119
Salmon with Chili-Lime Hollandaise, 115
Sandra's Express-O Cocktail, 233
Sandwiches
Bourbon Chicken Sandwich, 185
Captain's Club with Shrimp and Chipotle Mayonnaise, 144
Chicken Caesar Focaccia Sandwiches with Rosemary Skewers, 29
Creamy Chicken Mini Pitas, 29
French Brie and Ham Baguette Tea Sandwiches, 30
Olympic Hero, 198
Pesto Chicken Panini, 181
Roast Beef and Blue Cheese Tea Sandwiches, 30
Trout BLT, 131
Venetian Ham Panini, 101
Western Meatloaf Sandwich, 78
Sautéed Zucchini with Garlic and Herbs, 65
Scallop and Mushroom Chowder, 148
Seafood. *See Fish; Shellfish*
Shellfish
Captain's Club with Shrimp and Chipotle Mayonnaise, 144
Crab Cake Fritters, 22

Crab Parfait, 156
Crostini with Shrimp and Boursin
    Cheese, 25
Fettucini with Lobster Sauce, 38
Scallop and Mushroom Chowder, 148
Shrimp and Cheesy Grits, 136
Shrimp with Avocado in Tequila Cream
    Sauce, 135
Sicilian Steamers, 152
Tarragon Garlic Shrimp Skewers, 140
Shrimp
    Captain's Club with Shrimp and Chipotle
        Mayonnaise, 144
    Shrimp and Cheesy Grits, 136
    Shrimp with Avocado in Tequila Cream
        Sauce, 135
    Tarragon Garlic Shrimp Skewers, 140
Siam Peanut Slaw, 123
Sicilian Steamers, 152
Side dishes (breads)
    Chile and Cheddar Corn Muffins, 189
    Mozzarella Garlic Bread, 37
    Prosciutto-Wrapped Breadsticks, 46
Side dishes (grains and pasta)
    Black Bean and Spinach Couscous, 169
    Bulgur with Asparagus and Feta, 110
    Fettucini with Parmesan Sauce, 90
    Herbed Rice Pilaf, 128
    Mandarin Couscous, 119
    Nutty Herbed Rice, 174
    Soft Goat Cheese Polenta, 86
Side dishes (potatoes)
    Blue Cheese and Bacon Mashed
        Potatoes, 70
    Cilantro-Garlic Potatoes, 178
    Creamy Cheesy Potatoes and Broccoli,
        73
    Greek Garlic Fries, 201
    Ranch Mashed Potatoes, 165
Side dishes (salads)
    Arugula Salad with Pears and
        Gorgonzola, 50
    Balsamic Melon Salad, 101
    Black Bean Salad, 78
    Creamy Red Potato Salad with Green
        Olives and Capers, 132
    Fresh Broccoli Salad, 46
    Jicama Slaw, 135
    Minted Broccoli Slaw, 105
    Mixed Greens Salad with Fingerlings and
        Bacon, 116
    Mixed Greens with Mandarin Oranges
        and Walnuts, 37
    Peach Tree Slaw, 186
    Siam Peanut Slaw, 123
    Spinach Salad with Mangos and
        Mandarins, 151
    Warm Orzo Salad with Peas, Mint, and
        Feta, 162
    Warm Spinach Salad with Eggs and
        Bacon, 42
Side dishes (soups)
    Chilled Avocado Soup, 147
    Curried Apple Squash Soup, 205
    Fiesta Tomato Soup, 156
    Tuscan Tomato Soup with Basil, 182

Side dishes (vegetables)
    Balsamic Roasted Tomatoes, 57
    Beer Battered Onion Rings, 77
    Bourbon Creamed Corn, 94
    Broccoli with Almond Brown Butter, 143
    Creamy Cheesy Potatoes and Broccoli, 73
    Four Pea Stir-Fry, 173
    Garlicky Sautéed Green Beans and Peas,
        49
    Glazed Carrots and Snap Peas with
        Golden Raisins, 106
    Green Beans with Brown Butter and Pine
        Nuts, 124
    Green Chile Pintos, 98
    Haricots Verts with Shaved Parmesan, 38
    Lemon Artichokes and Capers, 155
    Maple Sweet Potatoes, 82
    Roasted Asparagus with Lemony
        Hollandaise, 197
    Roasted Asparagus with Portobello
        Mushrooms, 62
    Salad Bar Stir-Fry, 61
    Sautéed Zucchini with Garlic and Herbs, 65
    Spiced Zucchini, 139
    Spinach and Tomatoes with Feta, 193
    Zucchini al Formaggio, 53
Slaws
    Jicama Slaw, 135
    Minted Broccoli Slaw, 105
    Peach Tree Slaw, 186
    Siam Peanut Slaw, 123
Soft Goat Cheese Polenta, 86
Soups
    Chilled Avocado Soup, 147
    Curried Apple Squash Soup, 205
    Fiesta Tomato Soup, 156
    Scallop and Mushroom Chowder, 148
    Tuscan Tomato Soup with Basil, 182
Spiced Zucchini, 139
Spinach
    Black Bean and Spinach Couscous, 169
    Pork Piccata with Wilted Spinach, 89
    Spinach and Tomatoes with Feta, 193
    Spinach Salad with Mangos and
        Mandarins, 151
    Warm Spinach Salad with Eggs and
        Bacon, 42
Squash. *See also Zucchini*
    Curried Apple Squash Soup, 205
    Linguine with Vegetable Alfredo, 41
Starters and snacks
    Artichoke Focaccini, 26
    Chicken Caesar Focaccia Sandwiches
        with Rosemary Skewers, 29
    Chili Cheese Slices, 26
    Crab Cake Fritters, 22
    Creamy Chicken Mini Pitas, 29
    Crostini with Shrimp and Boursin
        Cheese, 25
    Fried Cheese Ravioli with Tomato Pepper
        Relish and Artichoke Caper Dip, 21
    Greek Layered Dip with Pita Chips, 18
    Prosciutto-Tied Asparagus, 25
    Tea Sandwiches Two Ways, 30
Steak House Salad with Horseradish
    Dressing, 74

Strawberry Creamsicle Martini, 233
Sweet Potatoes, Maple, 82
Swordfish with Ginger-Garlic Sauce, 120
T
Tacos, Carnitas, 97
Tarragon Garlic Shrimp Skewers, 140
Tilapia, Wine Poached, with Herb Sauce, 124
Tiramisù à l'Orange, 217
Toffee, Banana Pie, 221
Tomatoes
    Balsamic Roasted Tomatoes, 57
    Chicken Vera Cruz, 177
    Fiesta Tomato Soup, 156
    Fresh Broccoli Salad, 46
    Lamb and Olive Skewers, 109
    Linguine with Zucchini Caponata, 45
    Orecchiette with Sweet Red Pepper
        Sauce, 58
    Penne Puttanesca, 53
    Ravioli Balsamico, 62
    Spinach and Tomatoes with Feta, 193
    Tarragon Garlic Shrimp Skewers, 140
    Trout BLT, 131
    Tuscan Tomato Soup with Basil, 182
Trifle, Tropical, 218
Tropical Trifle, 218
Trout BLT, 131
Tuna
    Penne Niçoise, 50
Tunisian Turkey Salad, 202
Turkey
    Olympic Hero, 198
    Tunisian Turkey Salad, 202
    Turkey Cutlets with Cranberry Chutney, 194
    Turkey with Portobello Sauce, 190
Tuscan Tomato Soup with Basil, 182

V
Vegetables. *See also specific vegetables*
    Salad Bar Stir-Fry, 61
Venetian Ham Panini, 101

W
Walnuts
    Mixed Greens with Mandarin Oranges
        and Walnuts, 37
    Orange-Walnut Pesto Chicken, 165
    Ravioli Balsamico, 62
Warm Orzo Salad with Peas, Mint, and Feta,
    162
Warm Spinach Salad with Eggs and Bacon, 42
Wasabi Chicken, 170
Western Meatloaf Sandwich, 78
Wine Poached Tilapia with Herb Sauce, 124

Y
Yogurt Garlic Sauce, Lamb Chops with, 106

Z
Zucchini
    Linguine with Vegetable Alfredo, 41
    Linguine with Zucchini Caponata, 45
    Sautéed Zucchini with Garlic and Herbs, 65
    Spiced Zucchini, 139
    Zucchini al Formaggio, 53

Free
Lifestyle web magazine subscription

Just visit
www.semi-homemade.com
today to subscribe!

Sign yourself and your friends and family up to the semi-homemaker's club today!

Each online issue is filled with fast, easy how-to projects, simple lifestyle solutions, and an abundance of helpful hints and terrific tips. It's the complete go-to magazine for busy people on-the-move.

tables & settings	fashion & beauty	ideas	home & garden	fabulous florals
super suppers	perfect parties	great gatherings	decadent desserts	
gifts & giving	details	wines & music	fun favors	semi-homemaker's club

Semi-Homemade.com
making life easier, better, and more enjoyable

Semihomemade.com has hundreds of ways to simplify your life—the easy Semi-Homemade way! You'll find fast ways to de-clutter, try your hand at clever crafts, create terrific tablescapes or decorate indoors and out to make your home and garden superb with style.

We're especially proud of our Semi-Homemakers club: a part of semi-homemade.com which hosts other semihomemakers just like you. The club community shares ideas to make life easier, better, and more manageable with smart tips and hints allowing you time to do what you want! Sign-up and join today—it's free—and sign up your friends and family, too! It's easy the Semi-Homemade way! Visit the site today and start enjoying your busy life!

*Sign yourself and your friends and family up
to the semi-homemaker's club today!*

tablescapes   home   garden   organizing   crafts

everyday & special days   cooking   entertaining   cocktail time

Halloween   Thanksgiving   Christmas   Valentine's   Easter   New Year's